Comparative Philosophy

Western, Indian and Chinese Philosophies Compared

Revised Edition

ARCHIE J. BAHM
Professor of Philosophy
University of New Mexico

WORLD BOOKS

Albuquerque

First Edition: Copyright by Archie J. Bahm, 1977.
ISBN: 0-911714-10-3
L.C. No.: 78-10406

Revised Edition: Copyright by Archie J. Bahm, 1995.
ISBN: 0-911714-22-7
L.C. No.: 95-61792

Published by: WORLD BOOKS
Archie J. Bahm, Publisher
1915 Las Lomas Rd. N.E.
Albuquerque, N.M. 87106-3805
U.S.A.

COMPARATIVE PHILOSOPHY

CONTENTS

v

ACKNOWLEDGMENTS

Acknowledgment with appreciation is hereby expressed for permission to quote materials as indicated in the footnotes. Two acknowledgements call for special mention. Republication of "Eastern and Western Ideals, A Comparison," from *Darshana International*, Vol. XIII, No. 3, July, 1973, pp. 37-61, of which J.P. Atreya is Editor. Republication of "Standards for Comparative Philosophy," from *Philosophy East and West* (Presentation Volume in honour of Dr. T.M.P. Mahadevan, December 12, 1974), pp. 81-94, edited by H.D. Lewis and published by Blackie and Sons, Ltd., Bombay.

A.J.B.

PREFACE

Comparative philosophy is a relatively new field of study, research, achievement in understanding and teaching. The purpose of this work is to help clarify the nature of comparative philosophy; to survey views about the kinds of standards that may be used as bases for comparisons; and to propose an hypothesis comparing pervasive traits of the philosophies of Western, Indian and Chinese civilizations.

I

Comparative philosophy is not merely a comparison of philosophies. It is itself a kind of philosophy. In addition to minor varieties of comparisons, comparative philosophy achieves its maturity in comparing the major traits of the world's main civilizations. It has a subject matter of its own, not only the philosophies of the great civilizations but also problems relating to similarities and differences among them. It has its own values—added richness and variety of problems and solutions to work with, new insights resulting from new comparisons, more comprehensive and more adequate perspectives making truer views possible, and, if survival of mankind depends on achieving some minimum of a world philosophy to which all can subscribe, may serve as an essential instrument for the understanding needed for human survival.

Comparative philosophy has its own history of attempts at comparison. Sixteen such attempts are summarized as examples of initial efforts. Each has some merit, though each may be more significant as a prod for further research than as a complete or accurate comparison. Comparative philosophy includes several comparative fields: comparative religion, comparative aesthetics, comparative metaphysics, comparative logic, etc., each beginning to have a development of its own. As a new field of study, comparative philosophy is a new specialized area of philosophy. As such, some may see it as a new branch. But since the opportunities for obtaining greater richness of variety of insights, for comprehension of problems and solutions, and for fuller and more advanced synthetic challenges to understanding inhere in it, it can, and I believe it should, be regarded as the supreme field of philosophy. Philosophy as a comprehensive science, incorporating problems and conclusions of all of the philosophical sciences and of all social, biological and physical sciences, achieves its fullest comprehensiveness in and as comparative philosophy, provided the comparative philosopher utilizes his learning to achieve such comprehension.

II

The problem of standards for comparisons arises because each dogmatist can claim that he is a comparative philosopher when he compares other philosophies with his own for the purpose of depreciating their deficiencies. Objectivity as freedom from bias is desirable in formulating reliable hypotheses. Yet each beginner has only his own philosophy as his basis for comparison. One who succeeds in suspending judgment while pursuing comparative studies still faces questions about what traits shall be selected as bases for making comparisons.

Controversies rage over what policy is best to adopt regarding standards. Should one seek to make comparisons on the basis of all universal traits, all unique traits, all traits, or selected traits (e.g., those selected by previous comparers)? Some claim that there can be no standards. Some propose an ideal standard constructed from various suggestions emerging from studies. Some say we must await the emergence of a stable world culture before judging the relative merits of traits contributed to it. I do not propose a final set of standards, but I believe that comparative studies will be improved when attention is given to problems of diminishing bias and improving adequacy of bases for comparison.

III

A main purpose of this work is to present for criticism an hypothesis comparing philosophical ideas and ideals pervasively emphasized differently in Western, Indian and Chinese civilizations. Western civilization has a double heritage of ideals. Greek philosophers taught it to idealize reason. Hebraic thinkers idealized will, the will of God and the wills of persons. Augustine synthesized these ideals in Christian theology—will and reason are identical in God, who is perfect, but not in persons, who are imperfect. The history of Western philosophy has been characterized by controversies over the relative ultimacy of reason and will, and over their relative incompatibility or complementarity. Indian thought, despite its varieties, has tended to idealize intuition of ultimate reality as pure indistinctness and achievement of such reality through extinction of desire.

The two ideals, reason and intuition, are poles apart. The rationalist idealized definiteness and distinctness in existence and clarity and precision in understanding. The intuitionist dedicated to idealizing indefiniteness and indistinctness pursues yogic efforts to purify awareness of all contents. The two ideals, willfulness (desire) and will-lessness (desireless-ness), are poles apart. They are accompanied by opposing ideals: activity versus passivity, progress versus eternality, and production of goods versus non-attachment.

The importance of reason and will as Western philo-sophical ideals is clarified and brought home to Western philosophers by the discovery that their opposites, intuition of indistinctness and extinction of desire, are idealized in Indian thought. Some comparers interpret these opposites as contradictory. I choose to see them as com-plementary.

Chinese civilization appears to have embodied ideals present in the thought of Lao-Tzu and Confucius as divergent from Indian as from Western ideals. Discounting Buddhism in China as an import from India, we may observe that Chinese thinkers were not interested in press-ing their ideals to the extremes of perfection of definition versus perfection of indefiniteness and of willfulness versus will-lessness. Risking oversimplification, I propose that Chinese thought has tended to emphasize ideals of willing-ness as opposed to either willfulness or will-lessness, and ideals of distinctions (opposites: *yang* and *yin*) that are not completely distinct (Tao symbol diagonal incorporates both opposites). The *I Ching* is the Chinese masterpiece of logic, sixty-four hexigrams suggestive of types of analogies. The complementarity of opposites is a central emphasis in much of Chinese thought.

I believe that Indian and Western thinkers both have much more to learn from Chinese philosophy than most now realize, and that ideals emphasizing the complementa-rity of opposites have more to contribute to the needed emerging world philosophy than ideals emphasizing opposi-tion in terms of contradictory extremes. But my beliefs are tentative, exploratory and propositional. I have not been able to present here the quantities of data on which my hypo-

thesis is based. I trust that it will prove sufficiently suggestive and provocative to induce further studies in comparative
philosophy.

ARCHIE J. BAHM

PREFACE

Revised Edition

Revisions in this Edition consist, first, in eliminating pages 82-98 (Criticisms of Northrop's *Comparative Philosophy*, and Index), and secondly, inclusion of pages 82-103 (Chapters IV, V, VI, and a new Appendix). Chapters IV and V express an advance in my ability as a comparative philosopher. On August 23, 1993, I presented a paper, "Three Truths: Western, Indian, and Chinese," in the XIXth World Congress of Philosophy in Moscow. My Western perspective interpreted Indian and Chinese views in the Western language as "truths." Further study convinced me that a more adequate treatment requires stating the views of different civilizations in terms of their own concepts. Hence, Chapter IV, "Truth, Satya, Chéng: A Comparative Study," does this. Chapter V, "Good, Ananda, Chung: A Comparative Study," does the same.

The new Appendix, "Comparative Philosophy and World Philosophy," expresses my growing interest in World Philosophy and how Comparative Philosophy can serve it. Chapters IV, V, and VI present challenges to the quest for World Philosophy by emphasizing kinds of differences that need profound consideration.

I. WHAT IS COMPARATIVE PHILOSOPHY?

A. COMPARATIVE PHILOSOPHY IS PHILOSOPHY

What is philosophy? Fully comprehended, philosophy includes at least six fundamental components—problems, attitudes, methods, activities, conclusions and effects.

Problems about the nature, including origin, development and future, of self, society and the universe and their interrelations arise, naturally or artificially, in the minds of most people as they grow to maturity. Prolonged systematic efforts to deal with these problems have led to grouping them into problems of knowledge (epistemology, logic, philosophy of science, philosophy of language), problems of reality or existence (metaphysics, ontology, cosmology), problems of values (axiology, aesthetics, ethics, philosophy of religion) and problems of society (social, economic and political philosophy). The problems are so intimately and intricately interrelated that, no matter where one begins, he tends to be drawn into dealing with the others before he can find fully satisfactory answers to any one of them. A major problem of philosophy consists in how to fit all the distinct parts into a comprehensive whole. Increasing difficulties in dealing with this problem, as the knowledge explosion reveals a more complicated picture, have led to its neglect. But the problem will not disappear because like the others it grows out of life itself and out of the need which naturally arises of wanting to understand that life.

Attitudes toward philosophical problems are many, but only some of them are appropriately called "philosophical." Attitudes toward life untroubled by problems are not philosophical, except in that popular usage of the term which includes all of one's views about anything as a part of his philosophy. Philosophy as "love of wisdom" arises only after doubt has troubled one's confidence. Wondering about which view is true, being open-mindedly willing to accept whichever view is true, being willing to be guided by experience and reason and both to speculate about alternative possibilities and to suspend judgment in the absence of adequate evidence for achieving are all ingredients in the philosophical attitude. The moment confidence in one's conclusion becomes complete, the philosophical attitude toward one's conclusion has disappeared. One's religion is the practice of one's philosophy of life, and the thin and wavering line between confidence and uncertainty, conviction and tentativeness, faith and doubt is often hard to detect in oneself and in others. Paradoxically, the confident doubter (sceptic or agnostic) may live manifestly more religiously than the worried believer. Philosophy and religion are not two kinds of philosophy, as so many Westerners believe; and philosophy is not indistinct from religion, as many Hindus believe. Philosophy is a quest for understanding, so that one may live better; and religion is living what one understands. For those who learn to live by living, philosophy and religion develop together.

Methods of dealing with philosophical problems likewise are many, too many to explore here. Whether one struggles wildly, reflects logically, develops dialectically, alone or with others, achieving solutions to problems is what is important. Yet some methods seem better than others, at least for some people.

Activities in the minds of persons dealing with philosophical problems vary from one's first wonder about whether things are as they seem, through those of the tortured disbeliever, through those in philosophy classes and meetings in philosophical societies, to international congresses and professional think-tanks. They begin with a child's first query about whether things really are as they seem, and continue till death eradicates any final uncertainty.

Conclusions are philosophical when they are conclusions to philosophical problems dealt with by philosophical attitudes and methods. And the effects of such conclusions, activity, methods, attitudes and problems upon the lives of individuals, societies and civilizations are perhaps the most significant parts of what philosophy is and does.[1]

Comparative philosophy is philosophy in the foregoing senses. Its problems are a part of the problems constituting philosophy. On the one hand, its problems are the same in kind as the rest of philosophy, inquiring into the nature of self, society and the universe and into the nature of knowledge, existence and values. On the other hand, its special concern with comparisons gives it some additional problems, which require their own added emphases regarding attitudes, methods, activities, conclusions and effects. A main purpose of this essay is to explore, and to explain the nature of, these additional problems and emphases.

B. COMPARATIVE PHILOSOPHY IS COMPARATIVE

What is meant by "comparative"? Since the word has a broad range of meanings, even relative to philosophical problems and conclusions, the restrictions upon its meaning appropriate to our subject need to be made clear.

1) Broadly conceived, nothing in philosophy is older than comparative philosophy, unless we mean by philosophy any view one happens to hold no matter how intuitively or authoritatively acquired. If one cannot be philosophical without having a philosophical attitude, and if one cannot have a philosophical attitude without entertaining some

3

doubt, and if one cannot have a doubt about one viewpoint without implicitly, at least, entertaining the possibility of one or more alternative viewpoints, and if one cannot entertain such possibility without being involved in comparison in this sense, then, in this broad sense, all philosophy is comparative, for as soon as one is confronted with two or more alternative solutions to any problem, one is already comparing. And each person's own philosophy, if it has resulted from choosing among many such alternatives relative to various problems, is, in this sense, already very much a product of comparisons.

2) Whenever one encounters another person with a different philosophy, comparisons naturally tend to result. Problems of communication are complicated by using common words with differing philosophical connotations. Thus communication with others often involves comparisons.

3) Anyone who studies the history of philosophies within each civilization finds himself comparing the views of one philosopher with others, whether contemporaries, predecessors or successors. One might try to write a history of philosophies as a series of insulated views, but one would surely fail, because most historically-remembered philosophers developed their views by agreeing or disagreeing with their teachers and fellows. Historically significant philosophers have tended to acquire their problems and to develop their solutions as a result of comparisons with the views of other philosophers. Hence comparisons in these ways are a part of the history of philosophy. So comparisons by philosophers with the views of other philosophers are natural parts of the nature of philosophy itself.

4) Another meaning of "comparative philosophy" refers to comparisons made about the views of philosophers, or philosophical movements, in two different civilizations. The number of books, many of them doctoral dissertations, comparing two philosophers from different civilizations is already large. Such pairs as Jesus and Gandhi, Bradley and Shankara,

4

What is Comparative Philosophy?

Socrates and Buddha, Spinoza and Lao Tzu, Kant and Confucius, the Greek Atomists and the Hindu Charvakas, for example, are sometimes taken to exemplify not merely persons but types. Although the scholar's quest is for understanding, some betray a preference for similarities and others differences, for example, Dewey and Patanjali or Bergson and Mahavira. Such comparisons approach but do not by themselves achieve fully what we choose to mean by "comparative philosophy."

5) "Comparative philosophy," in the sense being clarified here, involves, as a minimum, comparisons of views from all the major civilizations of the world and, as a maximum, that is, as an ideal, comparisons of all views from all civilizations. From the perspective of the present writer, there are three major civilizations—the Indian, the Chinese and the European. So a minimum effort to function adequately as a comparative philosopher from this perspective will seek to compare traits in these three civilizations. Those who believe that there are only two major civilizations—Eastern and Western—qualify as comparative philosophers because they seek to compare all major civilizations, but are inadequate as philosophies because they mistakenly fail to recognize the magnitude of genuine differences between the Indian and Chinese civilizations.

There is still considerable range in the restricted meaning of "comparative philosophy" intended here, since it includes variations extending from comparing examples of the connotations of a single ideal (e.g., the future) in the three major civilizations, through comparing whole systems of thought (e.g., materialisms) in the three major civilizations, and comparing all of both similar and different traits pervading the three major civilizations (if any), and through comparisons including other, even all other, minor and minutest civilizations, regarding all traits. The range intended includes both comparisons of comprehensive perspectives and comparisons by special fields, such as metaphysical, epistemological, ethical, logical, etc. The range is intended to include comparisons made at some particular time in history as well as comparisons of histories of philosophies and their origins. Obviously, comparative philosophy so conceived is still magnitudinous, and is an area in which there will be much work to be done for a long long time.

6) Before leaving our varieties of meanings, let us look forward to still another meaning which may be expected to emerge if, indeed, it is not already functioning actively in the minds of many forward-looking scholars. If, as seems probable, some kind of world culture is emerging in which the philosophies of each of the civilizations are contributing some parts, then comparisons of such contributions will become possible. After the fact, it should become possible not only to assess the relative significance of the contributions from each civilization but also to evaluate those contributions comparatively, not merely relative to contributions actually made but even relative to their previous suitability to participate in the ways they do. The problems and standards, as well as possibilities, for making such comparisons may be somewhat different from comparisons made prior to the emergence of a world culture. The perspective of world culture will be available as a factor which is now missing for those making comparisons primarily from within one of the civilizations.

We intend the fifth meaning above in the remainder of this essay when we refer to "comparative philosophy" as "comparative."

C.   COMPARATIVE PHILOSOPHY HAS ITS OWN SUBJECT MATTER

Comparative philosophy is a distinguishable field of inquiry, with its own problems, its own attitudes, methods, activities, conclusions and effects. Disagreements about the precise limits of the field's boundaries may continue, even as it may also continue to grow in complexity and extent as its own history continues. But that there is such a field of inquiry in which investigators are actively engaged should now be obvious. What the scope of this subject matter is I shall try to outline.

Negatively, it differs both from non-comparative philosophy, from comparative studies of culture which do not involve philosophy, and from other kinds of comparisons noted in the previous section (1-4). It is not preoccupied directly with the solution of particular problems, such as the nature of truth or self or causality, even though it remains intimately interrelated with them, both because it depends upon them as data which serve as bases for its comparisons and because it may make contributions to their solution as a consequence of new knowledge resulting from comparisons.

Positively, it differs from the philosophies within each civilization because it does not come into being until comparisons between (ideally, all; minimally, the major three) different civilizations is under way. Its subject matter consists in the problems which arise as a result of making such comparisons. Although on the one hand it may appear to be not new in the sense that the philosophies which it compares already exist, on the other, new problems arise when one begins to compare, and these generate other problems which could not have been predicted prior to such undertakings. What are some of these problems?

1) First, the comparative philosopher in any one civilization must endeavor to understand the philosophies in each of the other civilizations. This involves the philosophies in the other civilizations being understood from an external viewpoint.

Problems arise when philosophies which have become culturally acclimated are suddenly exposed to questions that have developed part of their significance as a result of peculiarities in a different civilization. Under such circumstances, not only is the investigator from one civilization confronted with some new ideas but the philosophy being investigated is challenged by new questions. Thus, even from its very beginning comparative philosophy tends to involve a double catalysis—both the investigator and his own philosophical insights are challenged to change and the philosophies being investigated are infected with ferment if their proponents respond with competence, sensitivity and open-minded ingenuity. Comparative philosophy is a dynamic field which generates new problems as soon as attempts at comparisons begin.

2) Secondly, the comparative philosopher must try to understand the philosophies of the different civilizations together, that is, comparatively, first in detail and then more comprehensively. Obviously, this involves observing their similarities and differences. In what ways and to what extent are they alike and different? His task becomes complex and subtle as he explores differences among the likenesses and likenesses among the differences. The task becomes increasingly cumbersome when he discovers that similarities observed in two civilizations do not exist in a third, while similarities in the second and third do not exist in the first, and when an idea present in one civilization is absent from the other two in such a way that it functions as a significant negative similarity. Problems become provocative when several ideals fitting smoothly together in one civilization occur only as scattered fragments of diverse systems in the other civilizations. And the astonishing variety of combinations of ideas may appear to some as chaotic and as evidence for extreme cultural relativism on a grand scale.

But persistent study can reward the ardent scholar with several kinds of results:

a) It can reveal, because it already has revealed to several comparative philosophers, evidences providing bases for testable generalizations about prevailing tendencies within each major civilization. These philosophers have been able to develop theories about differing pervasive ideals which have tended to dominate their civilizations. A summary of some of their conclusions appears below (Section E).

b) A comparative philosopher may gain new understanding of the philosophies in his own civilization by seeing them contrasted with those in the others. I was able to discover that Western civilization has been dominated by concern about two kinds of ideals which are relatively peculiar to it only by studying Asian philosophies in which they were either ignored or despised.

c) A comparative philosopher may discover that the philosophies in different civilizations have a complementary character and that mankind has engaged, even if unwittingly, in a division of philosophical labor on a large scale. Problems continually ignored in one civilization have received intensive study and development in others. Types of solution regarded as unworkable in one civilization have been exploited successfully and elaborated to their fullest extent in others. As the fruits of comparative philosophy become more widely available, more people in each civilization can profit from the philosophical developments in the others.

3) Thirdly, the comparative philosopher must, sooner or later, face the problem, whether as temptation or challenge, of seeing the philosophies of all of the civilizations in terms of some kind of a whole. If he does not do so alone, then he will be urged to do so as soon as he becomes acquainted with the views of other comparative philosophers. This challenge has many aspects and may appear in several different ways:

a) Just to view the panorama of kinds of philosophies within each civilization fanned out as philosophies of kinds of civilizations begets a vision of great magnificence. Although one may pause in wonder and awe, as philosopher one can hardly resist inquiring what it is all about. Is there some nature to the whole?

b) Discovery of complementarity, interconnectedness, and increasing interaction among philosophies in different civilizations and awareness of their common origin, in human nature adapting itself in various environments, and common future, as possible ingredients in an emerging world culture, presents an intriguing puzzle which calls for solution.

c) Appearance of need for new efforts toward world peace on a shrinking globe which may be aided by reducing antipathies due to disagreements about presuppositions and ideals may grip the investigator with a sense of urgency to reveal the more basic structures underlying greater apparent diversities. Should not a Western comparative philosopher, acquainted with the Augustinian synthesis of Hebraic, Greek and early Christian philosophies, and with the Hegelian synthesis incorporating additional opposites generated through fourteen centuries of philosophical controversy as examples, be ready to grapple with the task of discovering some organizing pattern underlying Western, Indian, Chinese, etc. differences?

4) Fourthly, the comparative philosopher tends to be challenged also by the discovery that he is dealing with problems which no one has dealt with before. The newness here differs from that gained either within one's own civilization or by exploring the ideas in a different civilization, for it arises from facing conflicting issues originating from two or more different civilizations. Hence, the comparative philosopher·enjoys the privilege of achieving new insights which arise from dealing with his peculiar subject matter. Such novelty is of several sorts:

a) Not only are new problems generated as soon as comparisons begin (as noted in Section 1, above), but more, and more complex, problems arise as investigations proceed. For, when a philosopher probes the philosophies of two other civilizations regarding the same kind of problem, he not only may receive and give double catalysis, but also then try out the answers received from one civilization upon the philosopher in the other civilization. This kind of questioning tends to stimulate additional catalyses, not only in relation to both other civilizations, and in their relations to each other, but also the profusion of suggestions likely to result from continuing dialoguing may well generate new levels of insight in each of the three both i) about their own philosophies which would have been impossible without their mutual examination from partially external viewpoints; and ii) about higher and more general levels of philosophical interrelatedness.

b) Once this higher-level dialectical development is under way, it tends to evolve a nature of its own. New hypotheses are tried out and tested. These are not merely philosophies about philosophies. Comparative philosophy is not only "meta-philosophy," that is, philosophy about philosophy; it is philosophy about civilizations of philosophy. In becoming self-critical, comparative philosophy has among its problems the task of examining its own comparisons, its own philosophies of comparison, and of critically comparing its comparisons. Such a process of development tends to affect both the personal philosophies of investigators and the philosophical community, first among comparative philosophers who gradually develop their own corpus of issues and literature and then among others, including persons not primarily concerned with philosophy.

c) Experience with insights achieved at this new level gives some confidence that further study can reveal still more fully all of the presuppositions needed for an enduringly dynamic world order and how the seeming contradictoriness of some presuppositions will disappear as such high-level comprehension expands.

D.   COMPARATIVE PHILOSOPHY HAS ITS OWN VALUES

There are several.

1) The richness of variety of problems and solutions which

it inherits as source materials is greater than that of any of the civilizations which it compares. Including and transcending these civilizations endow comparative philosophy with both a broader perspective and greater quantities of details, and thus with additional opportunities for investigation.

2) The newness of problems and insights resulting from comparisons is of many sorts.

a) New insights into old philosophies can result from seeing them from new perspectives, challenging them with new questions, and subjecting them to new criticisms. Philosophies within each civilization so challenged may be improved. These may be challenges not only to particular philosophies and to many different kinds of particular problems but also relative to how to achieve comprehensiveness; for the task of being comprehensive has to expand to include the possibilities developed in the other civilizations. Each person as well as each spokesman for the civilization seems called upon to provide a grander vision than before.

b) New insights sometimes result when two philosophies come into contact for a first time. When their conjunction produces a third philosophy based upon both of them, a genuinely unique variety emerges.

c) A new higher-level field of investigation emerges as comparative philosophy maps out, explores, standardizes and develops the territory. The history of comparative philosophy and its achievements is added to the rest of philosophy. It, too, has its own open future and continuing developments to account for. This higher level may be thought of as a higher achievement by mankind, as well as by particular individuals.

3) The trueness of our views should increase as we become enabled to take more and more kinds of factors into account in reaching our conclusions. As we profit from the work of more philosophers in more civilizations, should we

not be able to achieve a more adequate understanding of the nature of things? If, as some believe, the more we know about ourselves and the universe the more we can do to make ourselves happy, then greater happiness should result from growth in comparative philosophy. If some say that the human mind is incapable of comprehending so much complexity, then this too is a part of the picture to be comprehended. Even though human minds do have limitations, we are far from reaching them; and we have evidence that we are able to extend those limitations through evolutionary as well as mechanical means.

4) The danger of human extinction by suicidal wars includes antipathies due to misunderstandings, some of them culturally induced. "This need to understand is no longer a matter of mere intellectual curiosity but of survival."[2] As I write, Volume 1, Number 1, of *World* arrives with Norman Cousins' editorial: "The issue is no longer what East and West can give each other but what both can give to the survival of civilization."[3] If comparative philosophy can help prevent human extinction, surely it has great value.

E. COMPARATIVE PHILOSOPHY HAS ITS OWN HISTORY

"Comparative philosophy is a new subject."[4] Although comparisons surely began as soon as travellers and scholars became acquainted with the philosophies of different civilizations, the arrival of self-conscious efforts on the part of professional philosophers to pursue such comparisons systematically may be of more recent origin. Absence thus far of any thorough effort to produce a history of such self-conscious systematic comparative philosophy leaves the field open for further investigation. But the fact that comparative philosophy has some history is obvious, for the titles of some books and names of some authors have already become familiar.

The following remarks aim not at an exhaustive or even adequate summary of such a history but merely to sketch enough to illustrate that historical development is already under way. References are limited to publications available in English.

Albert Schweitzer[5] contends that our will to live is experienced not only as volition but also as life-affirmation which begets reverence for life and attempts to understand life and the world. Westerners are inclined to assume such life-affirmation and world-affirmation as "more or less self-evident"[6] but are too optimistically satisfied with rationalized explanations which lack appreciation of the elemental will to live. The too-pessimistic Hindu "world view is based on world- and life-negation."[7] Though the world views of all three civilizations lack something needed for an adequate world philosophy, Chinese thought comes closest. "Nowhere has the problem of world- and life-affirmation. . . been felt in so elemental and comprehensive fashion as in Chinese thought."[8]

Paul Masson-Oursel[9] not only discussed problems concerning the methodology of comparative philosophy but also provided chapters on "Comparative Chronology," "Comparative Logic," "Comparative Metaphysics" and "Comparative Psychology," and ventured the thesis, regarding views of the nature of order, that "This order presents itself in Greece as a participation between ideas; in China as a hierarchy of values; in India as a classification of realities."[10] His penchant for uniformities led him to discover significant similarities amid seemingly extreme diversities. For example, he summarized, "Comparative philosophy teaches us that metaphysics exhausts all its efforts on this single yet two-sided problem—the double paradox of the absolute realized in ourselves, and of the imperfect created by the perfect."[11]

Charles A. Moore, organizer of the East-West Philosophers' Conferences (1939, 1949, 1959, 1964) at the University of Hawaii, editor of books reporting on those conferences,[12] and founder of the quarterly, *Philosophy—East and West*, in 1951 and its editor until his death in 1967, doubtless influenced the development of comparative philosophy more than anyone else while he lived. Yet he appears to have been more concerned with the development of mutual understanding and diminution of barriers to the synthesis of Eastern and Western philosophies as supplementary to each other than with elaborating a theory about differences.

Nevertheless, despite extreme caution in commiting himself to claims about a "distinctive spirit" of either Western or Eastern philosophies, he did offer two universal generalizations and five emphases. After criticizing ten claims characterizing Western philosophy, he asserted that "The only characterization that can be applied to Western philosophy as a whole...is that Western philosophy is 'determinate' in its concept of the real."[13] "In only one respect has the entire East reached unanimity of opinion within the field of our study. This is the view that all philosophy is ultimately for practical purposes...whereas Western philosophy as a rule is not."[14] The five emphases or tendencies in Eastern philosophy: An attitude of "Ultimate Perspective"; an attitude of "Dual Perspective," involving two levels in metaphysics and ethics, with an "initial pessimism"; a tendency toward some form of "Negativism"; Monism, or a tendency to see each person in some larger perspective; Spiritual-mindedness which rejects Western hedonism, naturalism and materialism.[15]

F.S.C. Northrop[16] interprets human experience as having two "ultimate and irreducible" components, the "aesthetic" or immediately apprehended (intuited) and hence certain, which is stressed in the Orient, and the "theoretic" or hypothetically constructed (postulated) and hence uncertain, which is stressed in the West. The "aesthetic," called "the differentiated aesthetic continuum," when taken in its

15

totality, includes two factors—the indeterminate, all-embracing, imperishable constant being, which is more elementary and primary, and the determinate, relativistic, transitory and varying phenomenon which is temporary and derivative. These two factors enable Asians to solve with assurance the problem of the one (indeterminate, eternal, all-inclusive, for example, Brahman or Sunya) and the many (determinate, momentary, differentiated, for example, Maya or Suchness) in conservative ways. The "theoretic," which involves inferred, not immediately observable, hypothetical constructs implying deductive consequences which can be verified only operationally, is characterized by tentativity, and lack of assurance, which is conducive to readiness to change. The two opposite and seemingly contradictory components stressed differently by East and West actually complement each other in ways such that both "concepts by intuition" and "concepts by postulation" may contribute harmoniously to an enriched emerging world culture.

Unfortunately, Northrop's understanding of Asian philosophies was insufficient for making clear genuine differences existing between Indian and Chinese thought. Despite complexities of different cultures, he claims that all of them together "possess inescapable identities" which "constitute a single civilization of the East."[17] "Jen in Confucianism, Tao in Taoism, Nirvana in Buddhism and Brahman or Atman or Chit in Hinduism and Jainism are all identified with the immediately apprehended aesthetic component in the nature of things, and with this in its all-embracing indeterminateness, after all sensed distinctions are abstracted. Evidently, Oriental civilization has a single predominant meaning."[18]

William S. Haas[19] describes "two separate forms of consciousness" which are "definitely not compatible and consistent."[20] "Unity in variety, the structural form of the Western objectifying mind, in the effort of saving—which is to say objectifying—the phenomena, reduces them to all-embracing thought so that at the ideal end of the process, thought faces itself. In the course of the realization of the structural principle of the East —juxtaposition and identity—the phenomena representing the Other are successively dismantled until at the end the identity of pure consciousness is achieved."[21] In working out details of his contrasts through thirteen chapters, Haas explores many East-West differences such as wonder *vs.* awe, love of wisdom *vs.* love of reality, desire to know *vs.* desire to be, preference for subject-object opposition *vs.* subject-other extension, interest in the objects of consciousness *vs.* interest in consciousness itself, time regarded as independent of experience *vs.* time as a flow of experience, critical attitude toward nature *vs.* confidence in nature, seeking to control body *vs.* not expecting to control body completely, and art work separated in ideal space *vs.* art work inviting spectator to cooperate.

Constantin Regamey[22] summarizes his inquiry: "The West is still, as always, animated by a creative power which allows it to attain its ends, but it has lost, or has not yet found, a universal ideal and is exhausting itself in trying to realize, with the same fanaticism, contradictory ideals; the East on the contrary has always been aware of the supreme and universal ideal, but it has not sought to realize it practically by adapting the world to that ideal."

Wilmon H. Sheldon[23] suggests three which are "not without exception." In the East, philosophy is a way of life, an experiment in living, a practical affair; in the West, philosophy is thinking about reality. In the East, philosophy is a search for the highest good; in the West, philosophy is examination and explanation of given facts. In the West, philosophy emphasizes the ultimate significance of time, process and progress; in the East, the progress-motive has not been typical.

O. Briere[24] says: "In a word, the Occident seeks the satisfaction of its desires, China their limitation, India their suppression."

Charles Morris[25] interprets statistical evidence gathered from questionnaires about seven "Ways to Live" as indicating preferences in the West for dominance, in China for dependence, and in India for detachment.

Huston Smith[26] recalls Bertrand Russell's claim that each man is perpetually involved in three kinds of conflict— against nature, against other men, and against himself—and identifies them with natural, social and psychological problems. Then he suggests, "Generally speaking, the West has accented the natural problem, China the social, and India the psychological."

Howard L. Parsons[27] asserts that "The Indians tended to seek to transcend the unity of man and nature through. . . identifying self with an embracing divine spirit. . . . The Chinese. . .sought to transcend the distinctions of the natural world by a human identification with the material source of all things, the great Tao of nature. . . . Western thought developed its peculiar dualism between body and soul, and between nature and man. . . .Western science has carried forward this dualism."[28]

Hajime Nakamura,[29] although not dealing "mainly with questions of comparative philosophy,"[30] does examine critically several theories about East-West comparisons in his extensive Introduction.[31] He concludes that "there exists no single Eastern feature"[32] and "as far as the ways of thinking are concerned, we must disavow the cultural unity of the West as we did in the case of the East."[33] Nevertheless, from his chapters devoted to Indian and Chinese ways, he demonstrates from linguistic usage and popular literature that Indian thinking tends to emphasize abstract and universal ideas and that Chinese thinking tends to be preoccupied with particular things and concrete situations and temporal, including historical, matters. His demonstrations do not extend to Western ways of thinking.

P. T. Raju[34] says "All the three traditions are thrown into one perspective, the perspective that develops from the standpoint of man as a conscious being with two directions, the inward and the outward. This seems to be the only proper and useful standpoint from which all the traditions can be viewed as philosophies of life. . .which are not and cannot be antagonistic when rightly viewed." Western philosophy is "primarily rationalistic and intellectualistic; and. . .overwhelmingly scientific and outward-looking."[35] "The main contribution of the Indian tradition is explication of the inwardness of man, the freedom of his spirit," "and through his very core to the Universal Spirit."[36] "The Chinese tradition is primarily humanistic" and "exhibits a pragmatic immediatism and is impatient with mere intellectual questions." "It is neither extremely inward nor extremely outward."[37] Raju recognized the importance of differences in Greek and Hebraic contributions to Western thought (Chs. I and II) and its diverse expression in Christian, Islamic and Marxist thought (Chs. VI, VII, VIII) in *The Concept of Man*, second edition. His professional concern for comparative philosophy led to his organizing the Conference on Comparative Philosophy and Culture on 22-24 April 1965, at the College of Wooster, where he teaches, and his editing a reportive volume, *East-West Studies on the Problem of the Self*.[38]

Alan Watts sums up three views of the world very simply: The West views the world as artifact (something made), India views the world as drama (something manifested), while China views the world as an organism (something grown). An artifact is made following a plan in the mind of a maker. In a drama (*Maya*) the actors play their parts as if real. In an organism the principle of order in the universe unfolds itself.[39] His Society for Comparative Philosophy is headquartered in Sausalito, California, in an ex-ferryboat.

Joseph S. Wu[40] sees Western philosophy as a "searching for clarity and certainty," which makes logic important, while "direct experience" is important to Oriental thought, which distrusts logic as a means to unlock the mysteries of the universe. The problems bothering Western philosophers "center about Nature" whereas those troubling Orientals "center about Life." "Nature provides more clarity and certainty while Life lies in the depths of vagueness and uncertainty." So Western philosophy is closer to science and Oriental philosophy more akin to literature and religion. "Western philosophers are highly critical while Eastern thinkers are considerably tolerant." Western philosophers "are more interested in the paradoxes of logic and language than in the paradoxes of human society."

I trust that my own, long in preparation, hypothesis about "Eastern and Western Philosophies Compared"[41] will be regarded as a significant contribution. Beginning with ideals emphasizing will, derived from Hebraic, and ideals emphasizing reason, derived from Greek cultural taproots, Western civilization, epitomized in Christian and later Jewish and Moslem theology, characteristically exhibits conflicts over their relative ultimacy. Despite more similarities than differences in Western, Indian and Chinese philosophies, comparisons reveal two main sets of differing emphases. Regarding will, the West tends to idealize willfulness, India will-lessness, China willingness. Regarding reason, the West tends to idealize definiteness, India indefiniteness, and China naturalistic analogy. These general emphases beget, and are supported by, multitudes of associated details. For example, willfulness is associated with encouragement of ambition and activity, progress and productivity; will-lessness with suppression of desire, passivity, eternality and withdrawal of attachment; willingness with accepting both desire and frustration and change and continuance as natural, being present-oriented and enjoyment. Likewise, definiteness is associated with understanding by analyzing parts, being realistic, seeking measurement; indefiniteness with intuition of wholeness, being subjectivistic, seeking yogic identity; and naturalistic analogy with apprehending participation, being naively realistic, and observing analogies.

I believe that the foregoing sample is sufficient to demonstrate that comparative philosophy already has its own history, even though the examples are limited to English language publications. Ignoring quantities of articles, I must mention that, in addition to theses about comparative philosophy generally, efforts to explore and develop theses about various branches of philosophy have begun to develop. The following are merely illustrative:

i) Philosophy of Religion. Probably more books have been written claiming to deal with comparative religion than comparative philosophy. We cite only the journal, *Studies in Comparative Religion*, published in Middlesex, England, since 1967, and one example—S. Radhakrishnan, *Eastern Religion and Western Thought*.[42] ii) Psychology. Carl C. Jung, *Psychology and Religion: West and East*,[43] Alan Watts, *Psychotherapy East and West*.[44] iii) Aesthetics. K. C. Pandey, *Comparative Aesthetics:* Vol. I, *Indian Aesthetics*, 1950, second edition, 1959; Vol. II, *Western Aesthetics*, 1956, second revised edition, 1972.[45] Pravasjivan Chaudhury, *Studies in Comparative Aesthetics*.[46] Thomas Munro, *Oriental Aesthetics*.[47] iv) Ethics. Kenneth Saunders, *The Ideals of East and West*.[48] v) Philosophy of Education. Ratna Navaratnam, *New Frontiers in East-West Philosophies of Education*.[49] If we add theories about comparisons made by historians, anthropologists, linguists, and other social scientists, the resources available to anyone concerned with the history of comparative philosophy are enormous.

F. COMPARATIVE PHILOSOPHY: BRANCH OR SUPREME?

I do not believe that a comparative philosopher need feel compelled to produce a comprehensive philosophy or to regard comparative philosophy as supreme philosophy.

But I do not see how he can avoid hearing the call to do so. One who does respond to such a call must go beyond mere comparisons. Yet one may believe that implications inherent in what he has found point so strongly toward comprehensiveness of vision and understanding that he feels forced to follow them to their natural conclusion. Whether or not a comparative philosopher does also seek a comprehensive philosophy, the problem is present and the challenge, for many, is urgent.

That philosophy is most adequate, or is supreme, which most fully answers mankind's questions about the nature of self, society and the universe, their origin, future and value, and how to maximize goodness. Surely a philosophy which is able to profit not only by the successes as well as failures enriching the histories of all of our civilizations but also by a history of attempts to compare those successes is better qulified to approach supremacy than those which are not. Let us trust that not only the comparative philosopher will respond to the urge to achieve comprehensiveness but also that anyone else who feels the urge to discover or produce a supreme synthesis will feel compelled to examine the evidences revealed by comparative studies first.

Disputes may continue as to whether comparative philosophy is merely a specialized branch of philosophy or is uniquely able to discover or create the most adequate philosophy. In either case, it is here to stay as a field for professional endeavor as well as a service to, and a remarkable achievement by, mankind.

NOTES

[1]For more details about the foregoing six components, see my *Philosophy, An Introduction*, pp. 1-31. John Wiley and Sons, N.Y., 1953; Asia Publishing House, Bombay, 1964.

[2]P. T. Raju, *Introduction to Comparative Philosophy*, p. v. University of Nebraska Press, Lincoln, 1962.

What is Comparative Philosophy?

[3]P. 2.

[4]P. T. Raju, *The Concept of Man, A Study in Comparative Philosophy*, 2nd ed., p. 14, Johnson Publishing Co. Lincoln, 1966.

[5]In *The Philosophy of Civilization: Part I, The Decay and Restoration of Civilization, Part II, Civilization and Ethics*, tr. by C. T. Camion, A. and C. Black, Ltd., London, 1923, 2nd. ed., 1929.

[6]*Civilization and Ethics*, 1929, p. x.

[7]*Ibid.*, p. ix.

[8]*Ibid.*, p. x.

[9]In *Comparative Philosophy*, Kegan Paul, Trench, Trubner and Co., London; and Harcourt, Brace and Co., N.Y., 1926.

[10]*Ibid.*, p. 121.

[11]*Ibid.*, p. 170.

[12]*Philosophy—East and West*, Princeton University Press, 1944. *Essays in East-West Philosophy*, University of Hawaii Press, 1951. *Philosophy and Culture East and West*, University of Hawaii Press, 1962.

[13]*Radhakrishnan: Comparative Studies Presented in Honour of His Sixtieth Birthday*, p. 86, Allen and Unwin, London, 1951.

[14]*Philosophy—East and West*, p. 266.

[15]*Ibid.*, pp. 281-317.

[16]In *The Meeting of East and West*, The Macmillan Co., N.Y., 1946.

[17]*Ibid.*, p. 312.

[18]*Ibid.*, p. 374.

[19]*The Destiny of Mind, East and West*, Faber and Faber, London, 1946.

[20]P. 284.

[21]*Ibid.*, p. 275.

[22]"East and West, Some Aspects of Historic Evolution," in *Transaction No. 6*, Indian Institute of Culture, Basavangudi, Bangalore, April, 1951, p. 17.

[23]"Main Contrasts between Eastern and Western Philosophy," *Essays in East-West Philosophy*, ed. by Charles A. Moore, pp. 288-297, U. of Hawaii Press, 1951.

[24]*Fifty Years of Chinese Philosophy*, 1898-1950, p. 28, Allen and Unwin, London, 1956.

[25]*Varieties of Human Value*, University of Chicago Press, 1956. See pp. 189ff.

[26]"Accents on the World's Philosophies," *Philosophy East and West*, Vol. VII, Nos. 1-2, April-July, 1957, p. 8.

[27]"Man in East and West, His Division and His Unity," *The Aryan Path*, January, February, March, 1961, p. 3.

[28]See also "The Meeting of East and West in Philosophical Thought," *The Philosophical Quarterly*, July, 1958, pp. 73-94.

[29]*Ways of Thinking of Eastern Peoples*, East-West Center Press, Hono-

lulu, 1960, 1964.
   [30]P. 9.
   [31]Pp. 12-38.
   [32]P. 21.
   [33]P. 24.
   [34]*Introduction to Comparative Philosophy*, p. 2.
   [35]P. 10.
   [36]Pp. 11, 15.
   [37]Pp. 10, 164.
   [38]Martinus Nijoff, The Hague, 1968.
   [39] See *The Book*, pp. 53-56, 115. Pantheon Books, N.Y., 1966.
   [40]"Contemporary Western Philosophy from an Eastern Viewpoint," *International Philosophical Quarterly*, Vol. VIII, No. 4, December 1968, pp. 491-497.
   [41]See Chapter III.
   [42]Oxford University Press, 1940.
   [43]Yale University Press, New Haven, 1938.
   [44]Pantheon Books, N.Y., 1961.
   [45]Chowkhambra Sanskrit Series Office, Banaras. Vol. III, projected, is devoted to details of East-West comparisons.
   [46]Santineketan, 1953.
   [47]Western Reserve University Press, Cleveland, 1965.
   [48]Macmillan, N.Y., 1934.
   [49]Orient Longmans, Calcutta, 1958.

II. STANDARDS FOR COMPARATIVE PHILOSOPHY

Now that comparative philosophy has become a recognized philosophical discipline or field, the question arises: What standards, if any, are needed by, or are natural to, worthy studies in the field? The problem becomes especially provocative when one hears an avowed sectarian declare that he is teaching comparative philosophy by demonstrating how other philosophies rate as deficient when compared with his own taken as the standard. And the problem becomes embarrassing when one who attempts to remain strictly objective in his efforts discovers that, unwittingly, he has failed, and that unsuspected biases have influenced his conclusions in ways which he had expected to avoid. A survey of some of the problems involved in trying to establish standards, and of some of the theories about such standards, seems worthwhile.

A. ONE'S OWN PHILOSOPHY AS STANDARD

Is comparative philosophy merely comparison of the philosophies of other cultures with our own taken as standard? An affirmative answer to this question has been given many times. Every ardent loyalist is likely to do so. Popularly at least it is the most common method. In fact, for most people, this is their only option. Usually a person is culturally nurtured within a particular society with its own world view.

If he knows only one philosophy, then when he meets another, he must naturally compare it with his own. If his own has been accepted as true, which is normally the case when no alternatives are presented, then he must judge the other in terms of what he already knows, and thus he must judge the other in terms of his own as standard.

Even after acquaintance with one or many other philosophies, a person may continue to accept his own as standard. There are many reasons for this. His first beliefs have become habitual, and habits are hard to break. His philosophical beliefs and habits are part of a larger complex of beings and habits which intermingle with the structure and contents of his language, the mores of his community, the culturally-conditioned social adjustment patterns in terms of which he relates to others, his concept of his self, and his hopes and fears about security, esteem, companionship, and success. He has vested interests in the truth of his accepted beliefs.

Furthermore, as long as he does not understand other philosophies from the inside, so to speak, or from having developed equally similar habits and vested interests in them, he is unable to appreciate how well they can function as standards. What Anselm said about Christianity is true of all philosophies: "I believe in order that I may understand." So long as one has not been able and willing to believe, that is, to identify himself as a believer of a philosophy at least to some extent, he lacks something needed to understand it fully. So long as one does not understand other philosophies adequately and appreciate their workability as well as he does his own, he cannot be expected to accept the others as standards on a par with his own.

Criticisms of this view have been stated many times. Comparative philosopher P. T. Raju puts the matter this way: "The philosopher who thinks that his own philosophy is the absolute model does not gain anything from comparative philosophy. He is already self-assured, and his interest can at the most be one of vain curiosity or self-glorification."[1] He recalls the clear and compelling reasoning typical of the dogmatist: "If the other philosophies say what mine says, they are unnecessary; if they do not say what mine says, they are false." (Attributed to the Moslem Caliph Omar of Alexandria.) If there are some unique truths captured in each of the world's philosophies, then surely one can seem warranted in being dogmatic about his own philosophy only if he is ignorant of such truths. Also, is he not doomed to remain ignorant of them so long as he retains his dogmatic attitude? Must he not be proclaiming a philosophy which is at least partly false?[2]

Not every advocate and practitioner of accepting one's own philosophy as standard is such an extreme dogmatist. Not only beginners, those who first become acquainted with other philosophies, but also those who have been questing in earnest for understanding of other philosophies, will have to study other views by comparing them with what they already know better. If one has achieved sufficient curiosity and a willingness to examine the claims of other philosophies open-mindedly, he is already doing all that can be expected of him until he does gain the insights needed to understand and appreciate them more fully. Furthermore, even one who has achieved considerable success in comprehending and appreciating other philosophies still makes his comparative judgments in terms of the view, albeit a much broader view, which he now holds.

Hence, in searching for reliable standards for comparative philosophy, taking one's own philosophy as standard may be the least reliable, it should not be dismissed entirely or too quickly. For i) one's own view may just happen to be the true, or truest, even though one is not warranted in judging so from one's ignorant, or partly ignorant, condition. If ours is indeed the best philosophy, then this is what we ought to believe, and it is what we ought to take as standard. ii) If mankind ever does achieve a true, or truest, philosophy, then one will have to take it as one's own, and as standard, if one would be true, not merely to oneself, but to objective fact.

B. NO STANDARDS

According to cultural relativism, standards for judgment are relative to cultures. That is, cultures differ regarding what people in them believe to be good and bad, right and wrong, true and false. And so, what is judged to be good, bad, right, wrong, true, and false depends upon the peculiarities of the cultures. A traveller from culture to culture should heed the ancient advice: "When in Rome, do as the Romans do." When in Rome believe as the Romans believe. When in Rome accept the standards which the Romans accept. Each culture is its own ultimate basis for judgment and thus for its own standards.

This means that since, or in so far as, cultures differ there are no standards common to all of them. Two or more cultures may happen to have some standards which are the same, but this circumstance is more accidental than providing a transcultural basis for comparison. The comparative philosopher, consequently, is at liberty to observe the different standards established in the different cultures, and any accidental similarities, but he has no transcultural basis for making judgments. He might observe that people in one culture do not measure up to the standards of another culture, but since the standards of the other culture do not apply in the one, such an observation is irrelevant for comparative purposes. Hence, the comparative philosopher who seeks a standard by which to judge two or all cultures cannot find one by studying the various cultures.

The situation is even worse when seen from the perspective of personal relativism. According to this view, each person is unique and has his own unique biological ancestry

and his own unique variety of experiences which serve as
the sources of his beliefs. John Locke, British empiricist,
argued that each mind is born blank and is stocked with
ideas as a result of his own peculiar set of sensory and other
experiences. He argued against religious wars because he
believed that no one person is justified in asserting that
another person's views are false since each derives all his
views from his own private experiences, which he regarded
as the only source of knowledge. This view leaves the comparative philosopher with no common ground, not even
cultural, which can serve as a basis for standards for comparison. Each individual may, as a result of his own experiences, develop his own standards for judging good and
bad and right and wrong; and he may believe that, in order
to be true to himself, he must follow them. But this view,
personal relativism, offers the comparative philosopher even
less hope than cultural relativism of finding a reliable basis
for comparison.

Finally, there are those who advocate momentary relativism. They argue that what each person experiences is the
present moment. What is past does not exist and what is
future does not exist. All that exists is what is present.
Whether advocating a Zen doctrine of momentariness, in
which one willingly appreciates whatever appears, or an
Existentialist doctrine of authenticity, in which each act of
will is authentic only if it willfully refuses to be imposed
upon by laws (physical, moral, legal, or logical), by the wills
of others, or even by one's own previous promises (acts of
will), nothing exists beyond such present moments which
can serve as a basis for standards. No standards exist. Comparative philosophy is a futile exercise.

However, if one advocates cultural relativism, personal
relativism, or relativism of the moment, then, is one not
advocating a kind of universalism, that is, that all cultures,
all persons, all moments, are such that no standards common to them exist? Implied in each view is the claim that

it itself be taken as standard and that any culture, person, or moment in which a standard is stated is deficient in terms of the standard which says that there are no standards? Do you not find the advocates of these views also saying that those cultures, persons, and moments are best which least claim, or imply, transcultural, transpersonal, or trans-momentary laws or standards?

C. UNIVERSAL TRAITS AS STANDARDS

Comparative philosophy originates from the discovery that there are different philosophies. Observing both differences and likenesses between the different philosophies, one seeks to compare them in some way. If they are completely different in any way, they have nothing in common in that way. If they are completely alike in any way, that way seems insignificant for comparative purposes. But if they differ with respect to ways in which they are alike, then we seem to have a significant basis for comparisons. Some investigators focus their interests first upon discovering ways in which all philosophies are alike and then upon observing how they vary in those ways. Each such recognized universal trait then functions as a standard. Each philosophy may be judged as better or worse relative to how it measures up to whatever norm seems evident relative to it.

For example, if encouragement of truth-telling is found in every culture, then the bearing of metaphysical, epistemological, axiological, religious, economic, political, educational, etc., portions of that philosophy upon such encouragement may be examined. If some portions of the philosophy entail inducements to lying, then inconstancy appears. If encouragement of truth-telling is a universal trait taken as a standard, then philosophies which do not also encourage lying appear superior, relative to this trait, than others which do. If the comparative philosopher is able to observe in how far every philosophy measures up to this standard, he may be able to discover some norm, average, or prevailing level relative to such standard. The problem of the extent to which people in various cultures practise their theories is another matter, although this problem too functions as a universal trait; and one not far different from truth-telling as a trait, for failure to practise one's acclaimed theories is itself a kind of lying (usually called "hypocracy").

Practical problems involved in this theory include a need for great tentativeness regarding proposed universal traits when observations of their actual existence are incomplete, difficult, or even impossible. Occasionally, interesting folk tales, including creation stories, spread from culture to culture without becoming a significant part of the other cultural complexes. When the philosophies of different cultures function as systemic gestalts, they tend to have a kind of consistency about them, so that, even when enduring inconsistencies appear, they have a kind of naturalness about them. Imported ideas sometimes find a home, become somewhat modified, and blend more or less consistently with the new culture. But sometimes they exist as mere accretions. Ascribing universality to such traits hardly serves the purpose intended in selecting universal traits as standards.

Although the question as to which traits are universal is one which should be decidable with sufficient empirical observation, the multitudes of cultures and subcultures and the quantities of traits are such that disputes about some may remain for a long time. Especially when universal includes past cultures, including prehistorical cultures for which no evidence of their philosophies remains, and future cultures in which new experiments are yet to be tried out, any claim about the universality of a trait must be accompanied with some doubt. New ideas arise for a first time in history. If these spread and become universal in the future, are they to be included, or must universal traits have been present from the most primitive human association? If the latter is true, then primitive cultures provide the standards by which all others are to be judged. But if development of new ideas is itself a trait, and one which some philosophies encourage, then it may be that later cultures and more complex philosophies measure up better when it is taken as a standard. When evolutionary development of traits itself becomes a recognized trait, then patterns of development, and philosophies of history, become data for comparative philosophy.

Although one may disagree with Clark Wissler about details of a universal culture pattern, the relative uniformity of physical, chemical, geological, geographical, astronomical, biological, physiological, psychological (physical, individual, social), sociological, economic, political, epistemological, metaphysical, axiological, aesthetic,[3] ethical,[4] etc., conditions and factors limiting and supporting human nature tends to limit and support what is possible regarding philosophies. The complexities of conceivability, the amazing capacities for remembering, and the fantastic intricacies of imagination provide a plethora of varieties of philosophy. But one who is dazzled by the multiplicities of varieties should not overlook the foundational uniformities. It may well be that the greater the variety the more difficult it is for the comparative philosopher to find the universals, and to be sure that he has found them. But that there are some uniformities in the nature of mankind, in the nature of the world in which mankind exists, and in their interactive and interdependent continuation, which serve as a basis for universal philosophical traits, seems, to me at least, a reliable hypothesis upon which comparative philosophers can operate. But that only universal traits should serve as standards appears to me to be quite debatable.

Standards for Comparative Philosophy

D. UNIQUE TRAITS AS STANDARDS

If, when observing different cultures and their philosophies, we find some unique trait or traits which one culture and philosophy alone embodies, or alone idealizes as a worthy standard, what is to stop us from using it for comparative purposes? If each culture, each philosophy, has something good which others do not have, it excels thereby. So, regardless of whether the peoples of other cultures are willing to have their culture compared with it and thus judged deficient, does not the comparative philosopher have an obligation to recognize its uniqueness and worth for what it is. If it is unique, or if it is unique in its emphasis, then the comparative philosopher, seeking to know and to state what is true comparatively, surely is forced to recognize such uniqueness or unique emphasis or excellence.

If many cultures have such unique traits, then does not the job of the comparative philosopher include discovering and recognizing each and every such unique trait, and to recognize its role, actual or potential, as a standard for judging in comparing philosophies?

Some unique traits are trivial, others important, some temporary, others more permanent, some localized, others more pervasive in a culture. If one seeks to compare cultures and philosophies as wholes, one will be more interested in those traits which are pervasive, persistent, and important, and will tend to ignore the trivial, temporary, and localized. But when comparisons focus upon some special field, such as aesthetics, philosophy of law, or logic, one may find what was considered trivial for comprehensive purposes becomes important for specialized purposes. Likewise, the discovery of something important for comprehensive purposes can lead to discovery of traits having unsuspected importance for specialized purposes.

Comparative philosophy is interested in differences as well

as similarities. Unique traits as standards are especially well
suited to the former interest.

E. SELECTED TRAITS AS STANDARDS

The actual process in which traits have been selected as
standards by comparative philosophers may be regarded as
quite haphazard. Comparative philosophy within each major
civilization developed before comparison of philosophies between civilizations became very significant. So, issues about
which persisting disagreements within each civilization, as
well as which persisting agreements within each, provided
the starting points for comparisons between civilizations.
Ideals about what should be eulogized and what should be
despised within each culture naturally receive consideration
when each is compared with others. And, additionally, the
ideas and interests of the particular comparative philosopher,
who may be a rebel rather than a loyalist to even the commonly agreed upon ideals of his culture, may receive special
attention.

Doubtless there are historical reasons for which philosophical issues and what types of solution are favored in
particular civilizations. Climatic conditions, such as heat and
cold, geographical conditions, such as mountains, plains, for-
ests, rivers, lakes and oceans, agricultural conditions, such as
whether corn or wheat, figs or oranges, goats or cows, can
thrive, and biological conditions, such as competition with
carnivorous animals, insects, worms, germs and plague, all
may influence both the origin and the survival of types of
philosophy. Both accidental and persisting conditions which
have influenced ideas and ideals have become part of the
philosophical mores of each civilization. Peculiarities in the
circumstances of the founder, so-called, who is more often a
transmitter with modification, and the presence and ability
of memorizers, who can comprehend and transmit the ideas

34

as well as the words, influence which ideals shall survive. Both failure to invent an adequate language and failure to communicate the details and the spirit of a philosophy doubtless eliminated some philosophies that were useful and significant in some historical circumstances and that might have guided people in each civilization to a healthier and happier existence had they survived.

The question of which traits have been selected as standards by the circumstances of history, including which seemed significant to the first, as well as later, comparative philosophers is something which can be studied now. At least those traits that some comparative philosophers have explored and discussed and used in making their own comparisons can be observed by examining their writings. Although occasionally a relatively isolated trait may appear to have significance for comparative philosophy, more often the traits of a culture intermingle more or less consistently in a system-gestalt. When this is the case, the comparative philosopher confronts the task of comparing systems rather than merely isolated traits. This task is more complicated partly because two or more cultures can be found to have similar traits, each of which appears to be consistently integrated in one culture, with what appear to be different and inconsistent traits from the viewpoint of the other culture. Thus a comparative philosopher may find himself confronted with an intricate maze of similarities and differences that make achievement of an ideal of clear systematic comparisons seem hopeless.

Although comparative philosophers must be expected to vary in their intellectual capacities and habits, in their loyalties to the conceptual precommitments acquired by being trained in their own peculiar culture, in their open-mindedness and ability to believe, at least experimentally, the ideals of other cultures, and in their willingness and ability to be objective in their efforts, some who are dissatisfied with difficulties in their own philosophies are more easily convertible to the ideals of a different culture. Thus, relative ease of convertibility of a comparative philosopher, which may be conditioned by the relative inferiority and superiority of the particular traits or complexes in the first cultures which he studies comparatively, may be factors which determine what traits become selected as standards.

Difficulties with any selected set, no matter how natural their historical development, appear when additional issues call for attention. As comprehensive, philosophy includes all of the problems which face persons who want to know about the nature of self, society, and the universe, their origin, values, and future. When students of philosophy press systematically for fuller answers to all such problems, selected philosophies that have failed to deal with any of them fall short. A comparative philosopher, whose interests and perspectives are conditioned by the culture in which he was trained, or even to which he has been converted, sees things with biased eyes. When comparative philosophy is guided by selected standards, much is omitted. Such omissions must be corrected before comparative philosophy achieves its full stature.

F. AN IDEAL STANDARD

In studying the conclusions of several comparative philosophers, I have found that, despite their desire to be completely objective, each one selected standards which revealed an unwitting bias favoring his own culture. This observation generated the ideal, which many have had, of rising above one's culture. If one can somehow study sympathetically all of the world's philosophies and then deliberately try to view them impartially from a viewpoint transcending all of them, then surely one would be able to view them without the bias of any of them.

Like others having this ideal, I zealously sought to be fair to the philosophies of different cultures by exploring in detail their seemingly different emphases placed upon common culture traits. Some traits, which were idealized persistently through centuries, partly through their varied functions in different philosophies within one civilization, were persistently despised through centuries, partly through their varied functions in different philosophies within another civilization. The intricate intermingling of such traits through their variations in different philosophies revealed a kind of system-gestalt into which numerous other traits were integrated, sometimes with modification. These additional traits then could be compared with similar traits in the other civilization to see whether and how they are integrated into its system-gestalt.

The more detailed my comparisons grew, the more confident I became that my conclusions were soundly based. Then, while lecturing to philosophers at Santiniketan, an Indian reminded me of what I should have known already. My long and detailed list of items used in making my comparisons revealed my Western preference for pluralistic ideals. An Indian, seeing all as one, Atman as Brahman, would have no need for such a list. He is perfectly capable of seeking and finding such a list; but without faith that a plurality of details can bring one closer to the truth about the universe and its many philosophies, he feels no need to do so. Obviously, the longer my list grew, and I expected it to grow still longer as my studies progressed, the more my conclusions embodied unwittingly a typically Western bias. I had failed at least so far as my ideal of trying to rise above my culture was concerned.

If no comparative philosopher can succeed in rising above his culture, where does this leave comparative philosophy? Must every comparative philosopher be biased even when he tries not to be? Should we study the history of comparative philosophies as itself a history of biases? In fact, is not the ideal of rising above one's culture itself a cultural ideal? Do all cultures have it?

Surely it was not present before people were aware that there were different philosophies to compare. And those philosophies which regard themselves as superior have no need for it. Should the comparative philosopher who desires to rise above his culture abandon the ideal when it is revealed as itself representing a cultural bias?

Before I say no to the foregoing-question, permit me to squirm a bit. If comparative philosophy as a field of inquiry is open to the use of the scientific attitudes and methods, and if efforts to be objective and willingness to be tentative regarding one's conclusions are essential to those attitudes and methods, then ought not the comparative philosopher try to be objective and tentative? My answer is yes. But my critics point out that science and scientific ideals are themselves peculiarly Western products. By urging the use of scientific methods I thereby do not rise above my culture but express its bias.

My next move is to recommend that at least some children, those who may eventually become reliable comparative philosophers, be trained natively in all, or at least all of the major, cultures. We are familiar with bilingual and bicultural families. Occasionally, three cultures intermingle in a child's native training. Why not deliberately seek to have more children acquire the essentials of each of several cultures so that, as they mature in each, they will have all of the biases already within themselves. This is hardly rising above one's culture, but rather a merging of differing cultural biases within one person. Can children be so raised? Will such a child, as he grows, make his own comparisons and either reject one or the other of inconsistent differences, evolve a new amalgam of his own, or conclude that culture is all relative? Must comparative philosophy await such experiments, which may fail?

I have two more proposals to make. They will be developed in the following sections. But here let me record critics' claims that they too reflect a Western bias. The proposal to accept all traits as standards will meet the criticism that it favors pluralism, extreme pluralism, and equalitarianism, extreme equalitarianism. The proposal to await a developed world philosophy as standard involves attribution of reality to history, something which eternalistic philosophies sometimes deny.

G. ALL TRAITS AS STANDARDS

The problem of overcoming bias and unfairness regarding selecting traits as standards can be overcome by accepting all traits in all cultures, including those which are unique, those which are universal, and those which occur only in some. Comparative philosophy is incomplete anyway so long as there are items of philosophy which remain neglected. If a comparative philosopher approaches his work with the view that each trait is as worthy of recognition as any other trait, then he will not begin with preferences as to which traits serve as more significant standards.

But, even ignoring the criticism that such an approach presupposes favoring equalitarian ideals akin to those fostered by cultures favoring democratic ideals, the comparative philosopher must face the claim of many, if not all, philosophies that it is superior to the others, or at least that some of its traits are superior to those of others. These claims are themselves traits which call for comparison. And observing the interrelation of traits, both with the life of a people and with each other in system gestalts, one finds that some traits actually are more significant in the lives and philosophies than others. So, although this method may recognize all traits as equally worthy of recognition as standards, it can hardly fail to conclude that they cannot be all regarded as equally worthy standards. When some traits do in fact appear to be more significant in characterizing a culture and do in fact yield more philosophical insight when used as bases for comparing, does not the comparative philosopher have a responsibility for searching out the more significant traits? However, if one starts with a willingness to examine all traits as standards, at least he does not begin with a bias which omits any. By being open to considering all traits, he may discover some highly significant traits which have been overlooked by those using other methods.

The criticism that trying to keep all items of all philosophies in mind is too much for any one person or even a group of people, or any one library or even a group of libraries, has considerable merit. But now, with the advent of data processing machinery and computers that can be programmed for numerous kinds of organizing and reordering of data, new potential for handling complexities of traits makes the criticism less warranted. A grid recording all of the different philosophical traits horizontally and all of the different cultures, or philosophies, vertically, can depict comparatively the distribution of different traits in the different cultures. Computers cannot evaluate for use, but, when properly programmed, they can provide data which make evaluations easier, and sometimes even rather obvious. I am not suggesting that a comparative philosopher can accomplish his task more easily by using computer technology, since the cost in time and money in designing an adequate program and in preparing (and modifying the data) for the machine may be greater than that needed for other methods. But, given both computer technology and enough time and money and patience, the approach to comparative philosophy that begins with all traits as standards, or at least as possible candidates for standards, remains a genuine possibility. If and when relatively complete induction is available, we should be able to achieve greater assurance about conclusions.

Standards for Comparative Philosophy

H. DEVELOPED WORLD PHILOSOPHY AS STANDARD

If a world culture, and a world philosophy, emerges as a result of historical processes, then the comparative philosopher will be able to observe "the judgment of history." At present, questions about whether and when a world culture will emerge, and what it will be like, can be only speculative. But after a world philosophy does emerge, if it does, then it can be used as a basis and standard for judging the contributions by the various civilizations to it. Although such "judgment of history" does not rise above the various cultures, the different ways and degrees in which traits from the various cultures constitute a more or less consistent world culture can tell us something about them as actualizations of potentialities for such participation.

However, this kind of standard is different in kind from those previously considered. Of course, after it has arrived, the factuality of existing traits may serve as a stable basis for judgments. But for comparative philosophers at present, it remains merely a speculative ideal, and one that is not available at present as a usable standard.

Even without its presence, we can foresee criticisms of it. If a world philosophy does actually evolve, will it then be static or evolutionary? If evolutionary, then at what stage in its evolution should it be taken as standard, for some traits emphasized in one culture may be neglected in the first stages of such evolution only to become emphasized in a later stage. If some of the philosophical·riches of any culture are neglected in a world philosophy, the comparative philosopher may feel compelled to call attention to such neglect, and he may wonder what the world culture would be like if the neglected rather than the accepted traits had achieved embodiment due to different circumstantial causes. But now I reveal further my Western biases by being concerned about what may become and about what might have been. Giving credence to judgments about possibilities, to statements made with a subjunctive tense, is a practice emphasized in Western philosophies. Such practice may die out if mankind ever achieves feelings of greater certainty about its knowledge of the way things are actually.

Will not only philosophy but, more specifically, comparative philosophy finally achieve maturity? Do standards used by comparative philosophers evolve so that, when later philosophers learn from the mistakes of earlier ones, gradual improvement occurs? If so, will there come a time when this process culminates and some finally best standards will come to be commonly recognized among comparative philosophers? If so, then such standards can be used for comparisons. But again, for the present, such possible culmination remains an impractical ideal.

I. PREVIOUSLY COMPARED TRAITS AS STANDARDS

Having found fault with all of the foregoing proposals, I may be expected to offer some more positive suggestions. First, let me say that each proposal mentioned was regarded as worthy of mention and that, except for the proposal that there are no standards, I favor each as having something to contribute to the picture. I refrain from speculating how one might obtain a synthetic standard by combining the virtues of all of them. But each is worthy of further consideration.

As, perhaps, a more practical suggestion, which is not without its difficulties and faults also, let us examine the proposal that comparative philosophers consider the standards for comparison advocated by previous philosophers. This proposal may be both closer to the actual practice among comparative philosophers today and become practised more as comparative philosophy becomes more professionalized.

We can observe how comparative philosophers behave as they go about their work. Although some may come to comparative philosophy only after immersing themselves in the various cultures, some people become interested in comparative philosophy by becoming acquainted with what one or more comparative philosophers have done. In fact, discovering a book on comparative philosophy may lead a person to become interested in the various cultures for a first time. Once interest in comparative philosophy has been aroused, then a search for other comparisons is natural. If the order in which attention is given to such standards results from accidental or random factors, then this is another method of "selected traits as standards," except that now the selection is done by the accident of reading previous comparative philosophers rather than by observing which traits have become dominant in a culture, or have been acclaimed as superior by the adherents of a culture.

Any thorough student of comparative philosophy will seek out the works of others and examine their proposals. So, although he too may favor or disapprove proposals by others for his own peculiar reasons, the more such thoroughness prevails, the more the standards proposed by previous comparative philosophers will receive consideration. Any one who has a standard to propose will do well to compare it with the standards previously proposed. They can provide a kind of test in the sense that attention to arguments for and against them can serve as factors to consider in evaluating the relative adequacy of his own proposal.

A danger inherent in this concluding proposal is that comparative philosophy, like many other fields, may develop stereotypes relative to which previously considered standards remain worthy of recognition and which do not. Or, controversies about standards may develop and persist, with antipathies causing rationalizations that protagonists carry to extremes. But, regardless of such common dangers, it does appear that, as comparative philosophy grows in importance, at least some of the standards proposed by previous comparers will receive increasing attention.

NOTES

[1]*The Concept of Man*, second edition, p. 18, Johnson Publishing Co., Lincoln, Nebraska, 1960, 1966.

[2]For further discussion of the issues at stake here, see my *The World's Living Religions*, pp. 9-13, Dell Publishing Co., N.Y., 1964; Southern Illinois University Press, Carbondale, Ill., 1971.

[3]See my "Is a Universal Science of Aesthetics Possible?" *Journal of Aesthetics and Art Criticism*, Vol. XXXI, No. 1, Fall, 1973, pp. 3-7.

[4]See my *Ethics as a Behavioral Science*, Ch. IIff. Charles C Thomas, Springfield, Illinois, 1974.

III. EASTERN AND WESTERN PHILOSOPHIES COMPARED

The first thing to make clear in distinguishing between Eastern versus Western philosophy is that the prevalent language conveys a fundamental mistake. There are not two but three major historical civilizations, the Indian, the Chinese and the European, and two of these are in Asia. The task of this essay is to compare ideals which have prevailed in Indian, Chinese and European cultures.[1]

A second observation is that, although comparisons should involve examining both likenesses and differences, we tend to stress the differences and ignore the likenesses. People all round the world are, I believe, more alike than different, both biologically and culturally. But differences attract more attention. This essay will be devoted to proposing a theory about differences. Yet all of the traits which we shall be discussing are human; that is, they all arise from, or within, human nature and are such that peoples in all parts of the world could develop them if exposed to them in the same way.[2] In fact, most, if not all, of the traits can be found within each civilization. What distinguishes the three major civilizations from each other is the emphasis which is given to idealizing some traits rather than others and, consequently, for ignoring, suppressing, or even despising some traits rather than others. The hypothesis presented here claims only that some traits have received more emphasis than others, but that such emphases have proved significant in ways which make the cultures seem unique.

A third caution for readers is to beware of how true statements can be when they purport to summarize the ideals of millions of people for almost two thousand years. The ideals mentioned are uniform neither throughout a population nor throughout a history. The same ideal, even one which dominated a culture during some periods in its history, has been repudiated in other periods. Intermingling of cultures, obviously more quantitative in recent times, occurred also earlier, perhaps even from earliest times. Hence debates will continue as to the actual origins of the ideals which now seem to have received peculiar emphases in each culture. The more intricately one studies the details of life of particular persons or of particular times, the more likely, perhaps, is he to despair of ever finding bases for broad generalizations about persisting cultural traits.

Yet, as persons become more familiar with broad sweeps of cultural histories, persisting differences in emphases do stand out sufficiently so that they can be observed, generalized about and compared. The two traits which I shall single out for attention in characterizing European culture were not obviously European until after I had studied Asian thought and had found that these traits were not only not idealized but also despised. I had assumed that they were human traits, which they are, and that therefore they naturally would receive similar recognition in all cultures. Idealization of their complete extinction from experience and existence by Hindu thinkers opened my eyes to how significant they have been in influencing the actual course of European theory and practice. Having been forced to recognize not only the extremes of opposition which Indian and European ideals have reached, but also how thoroughly these ideals have penetrated all aspects of philosophy (metaphysics, epistemology, axiology, aesthetics, ethics, political and social philosophy, logic, philosophy of religion, philosophy of education, and philosophy of science) and religious, medical and social practices, I could not but accept the fact of pervasive differences.

The important issue then became not whether such emphases persist, but how many and which ones. I was both helped and hindered by discovering that others have recorded observations about such differences. A survey of theories about East-West comparisons yielded considerable diversity, as well as some penetrating insights. My own study continued for many years as a teacher of Asian and comparative philosophy. And my hypothesis, though endebted to many suggestions by others, has a structure and conclusion for which I am primarily responsible.

A fourth issue conditioning the present effort has to do with ideals versus practices. When we compare their practices with our ideals, their practices appear deficient. And when they compare our practices with their ideals, our practices appear degraded. Fairness requires equivalent comparisons, so far as possible. So the hypothesis presented here is intended to be limited to a comparison of ideals.

Although I had hoped that my extended studies in Indian and Chinese as well as European philosophies would enable me "to rise above my culture," and to present an unbiased hypothesis, criticisms by Asian audiences made me realize how much I had failed. Hence, I present my hypothesis as one expressing a European point of view. I begin with a quick review of European history. Despite all its diversity, European thought has been dominated, first by the development of, then the prevalence of, and then attacks upon the monotheistic philosophy shared by Christianity, Islam and, to a lesser extent, Judaism. For convenience, I shall focus upon Christianity, which took its relatively permanent shape in the mind of Augustine, perhaps more than in any other single mind. Christian philosophy (and later both Islamic and Jewish philosophy) has two major cultural taproots. One is Hebraic; the other Greek. Each had its own dominating ideal.

Hebrew thought, the early history of which is available to Jews through the Torah and Talmud and to Christians as the Old Testament, includes a development of ethical monotheism from polytheism through henotheism, and a god of many nations, to a god of the whole world. The conception of God (Yahweh), gleaned from various passages, combines the characteristics of an invisible nature power with those of a tribal chieftan. From the beginning until today, Jews conceive God as a person with desires, wants, wishes. Nothing is more obvious in such a conception, and in the advice ("laws") given for guiding human behavior, than that God wills, and thereby has a will or is a will. A creation story states that God produced the world by a series of acts of will. For example, "Let there be light; and there was light." Each person too has a will, and is free to sin. To "sin" is to will to go against the will of God. God, who desires what is best for men, not only hates iniquity and punishes justly but also loves and forgives mercifully. The point I am stressing is that will is idealized as essential to the nature of both God and man and thus is a fundamental ingredient in ultimate reality.

Greek thought, epitomized in the philosophies of Plato and Aristotle, emphasized reason (logos) as form, order, regularity and law, not only as the form of things and the order in processes, but also as timeless patterns of things subsisting eternally prior to their embodiment in the creation of existing things (Plato) or as unchanging forms of things (that is, "essential" versus "accidental" forms) which come in fixed species (Aristotle). These real forms of real things can be known. When the form of a thing occurs also in a mind, that mind has "in-form-ation." Science, or gaining such knowledge about the nature of things, is an ideal which developed in Western civilization primarily as a result of Greek faith in the logical structure of reality and its knowability by man. Man can know nature because man is a rational animal whose nature (logos) is akin to, or rather a part of, the nature (logos) of nature (what exists). Thus reason, broadly conceived to include both rational structures (forms, patterns, laws) and processes (inference, deduction, proof) is something ultimate. Both nature and man (and any God, for example, Prime Mover, which there may be, or must be) are inherently rational. Reason, in this sense, is present in, and even constitutes, ultimate reality.

Although Greek thinkers grappled with issues involved in reason and will as conflicting tendencies in human nature (for example, Apollonian and Dionysian behavior) and in the universe, idealization of a fixed, rational order of things tended to predominate, especially among the ideals which have most influenced European civilization. One Greek philosopher has asserted that, in all of the works of Aristotle, the Greek word of "will" does not occur. Doubtless Greek has more than one word for "will," but the claim illustrates a tendency which functions as a prevailing ideal. Although Jews reason and Greeks will, the notion of timeless forms was foreign to Jewish thinking, and though Jews had ideas of everlastingness, they had no idea of a non-temporal eternity until influenced by Greek thought. The Hebrew God was a "law-giver," his laws came into being by his acts of will; they were not conceived as subsisting eternally as something which he, like Plato's Demiurge, was forced to take into account when creating the world. Hence, according to the hypothesis presented here, European idealization of reason has its historical sources primarily in Greek philosophy and European idealization of will has its historical source primarily in Hebraic thought.

.Christian thought, or at least Christian theology, achieved its typical formulation in the mind of Augustine. Inheriting three centuries of controversial development regarding interpretations of the teachings of Jesus, Paul and other gospel writers, and Old Testament revelations, Augustine organized Hebraic, Greek and Christian ideals into a workable synthesis. Reason and will are in complete harmony in God, who is perfect, but not in man, who is imperfect. God always wants what is reasonable and whatever is reasonable God automatically wants. Sin, which is willing to go against the will of God, is interpreted as due to human deficiency, something required by the necessities of creation. Greek (Platonic) idealization of what is perfect as timeless was accompanied by the explanation that whatever is created in time must be imperfect. But Hebraic ideals of God as merciful as well as just necessitated a plan for saving imperfect mortals from the deserts of imperfection. Hence a doctrine of grace (saving even those who do not deserve to be saved) flows naturally from God (Jesus' Heavenly Father) as a God of love.[3]

Ingenious as Augustine's synthesis was, the imperfect harmony between reason and will in human nature led to increasing divergences regarding ideals. In medieval times, Thomas Aquinas, who, when he became acquainted with the writings of Aristotle, dubbed him as "The Philosopher," asserted the primacy of intellect (reason) over will in both God and man. But he was opposed by Duns Scotus who reversed this order. The Protestant Reformation found John Calvin, who interpreted God as predestining man by rational necessity, opposed by Martin Luther, who interpreted the doctrine of "total depravity" as implying that man is incapable of understanding the rationale of God's plan and so had to accept faith in God's grace as an act of will.

Modern philosophy, beginning with Descartes and running through Leibnitz, Spinoza and Kant, at least, emphasized philosophy as rational inquiry. The chief issues revolved about whether reason or experience (rationalism versus empiricism) are the primary, or even exclusive, sources of knowledge. But romanticism, spurred by Rousseau, developed by Fichte, Schelling and Schlegel, received expression in British romantic poetry and, mildly, in the writings of Ralph Waldo Emerson. Sentiment, ideals inspiring, and inspired by, our feelings, wishes, desires, not only arouse our enthusiasm but sustain our vitality. Reasons, whether logical, moral or legal, which restrict or inhibit willful self-expression are evil Logical Positivism, continuing the rationalist-empiricist debate by its emphasis on the *a priori-a posteriori* distinction, dismissed value judgments and acts of will as non-factual and thus as meaningless. But Bergson (elan vital) and Freud (libido) restored will to a central position in man and the universe (God can be conceived as Cosmic Libido). Current conflicts between linguistic analysts (for whom the goal of philosophy is to clarify the meanings of words) and existentialists (for whom *existenz*, each act of will, precedes *essence*, or what one wills) represent the continuing presence of the reason-will controversy.

Nothing is more typical of European philosophy than this recurrent debate over which is more ultimate in man and nature, or in experience and existence, reason or will.[4] Yet how typical it is will become clear only after we have surveyed the ways in which Asian philosophies show indifference to or antipathy to both reason and will.

For convenience, the following treatment will be divided into two main parts. The first focuses attention upon will, and compares Hindu and Chinese ideals in relation to European ideals. The second explores various issues related to reason, and makes similar comparisons.

WILL

Differing emphases can be summarized succinctly: Europeans idealize willfulness. Hindus idealize will-lessness. Chinese idealize willingness.

Despite its obvious oversimplification, the foregoing summary captures something fundamental about persisting emphases which participated in shaping the minds of peoples for many centuries. Each tradition has its own history of disagreements about the nature, causes, kinds and degrees of ultimacy of such willfulness, will-lessness and willingness.

But despite these disagreements, historical variations and the presence of counter-emphases at times, each civilization has exhibited a relatively persisting preference for the three differing ideals.

Stating the three emphases so succinctly does not do justice to the intricate varieties of ways in which these most general ideals manifest themselves in more specific kinds of ideals. The following paragraphs are devoted to indicating some corollary ideals for each of the three general emphases. These corollaries may be interpreted either as more specific examples of such very general ideals, as implications of them (such that if the general is present, such specific applications naturally follow), or as supporting evidence in the sense that each specific kind of ideal serves as further evidence of the prevalence of the ideal as general. All three interpretations seem appropriate.

1) Europeans approve encouraging desire. Hindus approve suppressing desire. Chinese approve accepting desire.

Why is desire encouraged in European culture? Desire is the source of satisfaction. Without desire there can be no satisfaction. Satisfaction is good. Therefore desire is good. Hence, encourage desire. Want what you do not have. Be interested. "Man can have nothing but what he strives for."[5] Advertizing is good. Why? It stimulates desires. Desiring is lauded in a popular song: "If you don't have a dream, how are you going to have a dream come true?" Some find inspiration in carrying the ideal to extremes: another song eulogizes striving "to reach the unreachable stars."

Why is desire discouraged in Hindu culture? Desire is the source of frustration. Without desire there can be no frustration. Frustration is evil. Therefore desire is evil. Hence, seek to eliminate desire. Orthodox Hindu philosophies and Theravada Buddhism seek to eliminate desire completely. Yogic practices include separating self from desire-stimulating sources by going into seclusion in a forest or cave, withdrawing attention from sensuous objects, stilling the mind by emptying it of all desirous thinking, and evacuating awareness of self, the agent which desires. Gotama, the Buddha, who advocated eliminating only those desires which will not be satisfied,[6] was regarded as a heretic. Advertizing, of course, is evil.

Why is desire accepted in Chinese culture? What is natural is good.[7] Desire is natural. Satisfaction is natural. Frustration is natural. All are good. Hence, neither stimulate desire which you do not have nor suppress desire which you do have. Neither encourage nor discourage ambition. Advertizing is unnecessary.

2) Europeans encourage activity. Hindus encourage passivity. Chinese accept the need for both, each in turn.

Why encourage activity? To will, or to desire, is to act. To act is to be alive. To act willfully is to influence or cause. To be will-less, desireless or inactive is to be dead. To will is to act as an agent. Free will and its exercise is important in life. Have initiative. Be inventive. Create. Implicit in this view is the notion that doing is more important than being. Pragmatic behaviorism says: "A thing is what a thing does." If there is no doing, then there is no thing. Children, and perhaps youths and adults, often approach a weekend with the view: What shall I do? If there is nothing to do, it is just like not being anybody. Elizabeth Gregg has responded to this common need by authoring a book, *What to Do When "There's Nothing to Do."*[8]

Why encourage passivity? If ultimate reality (whether conceived as *Nirguna Brahman* of Advaita Vedanta or *Purusha* of Samkhya and Yoga philosophies) is pure quiescence, then anyone who seeks what is most ultimate within himself can realize it only in such perfect quiescence. Being is more important than doing. Being is timeless. Action is temporal, temporary, and illusory. Therefore seek to be passive. If one cannot seek passivity without doing so actively, then he must act. But that action which is least active, and that "action which is in inaction,"[9] brings one closer to the goal. The paradox involved in acting passively is recognized by every major Indian school.[10] It is related to another paradox involved in idealizing a perfectly quiescent being imperfecting itself through disturbances. But, having idealized the perfectly quiescent being as most ultimate, one feels compelled to reduce disquietude and to encourage passivity.

Why accept both activity and passivity, each in turn? Observe everyday experience. There is a time to arise and a time to go to bed, a time to work and a time to rest. The sun rises, and the sun sets. Initiation of activity is symbolized by *yang*. Completion of activity or rather achieving of passivity is symbolized by *yin*. Every being (*ta*) consists of both *yang* and *yin*, both beginnings and endings, both initiations and completions, both activation and pacification. And being (*Tao*) is nothing apart from doing (*yang* and *yin*) and doing (*yang* and *yin*) are nothing apart from being (*Tao*). Being and doing are equally important, equally natural, equally good. Lao-tzu is quoted as saying, "The way to do is to be." It turns out that what he means is that each person should be himself, act in accordance with his own nature, rather than actively meddling in the affairs of others. Although one should accept both activity and passivity, each in turn, one should not be either over-active (act upon, and interfere with the lives of others) nor under-active (remaining passive, for example, in bed, when it is time to be active, for example, get up in the morning).

3) Europeans idealize being progressive. Hindus idealize being eternal. Chinese idealize being present-oriented.

Why idealize progress? To will, or to desire, is to lack what one wants or desires. What is lacking can be filled only in the future. So whoever wills or desires is future-oriented. Why? Because the satisfaction and fulfillment which are not present can be achieved only in the future. Hence we come to expect that what is future will be better than what is present. These expectations are reflected in the beliefs of those who expect children to be better than their parents, those who expect Heaven (future life) to be better than Earth (present life), and those who expect utopia, or retirement, to be better than present working conditions. Happiness, these views imply, is located in the future. Therefore work for it. A Lubbock, Texas, matress factory advertized its product: Buy our matress and speed your sleep. When Hindus take leave of each other, they place palms together and pause in silence for respect. When Texans depart, they say "Hurry back."

Why idealize being eternal? If the ultimate reality of self and the universe is timeless being, and time is not merely temporary but illusory, then what good is there in being concerned with time or with things in time? Such ultimate reality (*sat*, *chit*, *ananda*) is also awareness of ultimate value. Although Hindus have adapted their philosophy of values in practical ways, and recognize four normal kinds of value in life (*kama*, desire; *artha*, possessions; *dharma*, duty; and *moksha*, liberation), the greatest of these is liberation from time, from the seemingly endless rounds of reincarnation pervaded with activity, and anxiety. The goal is eternal peace, quietude, passivity (*nirvana*). The eternal can be apprehended only in intuition. Withdraw from progressive, acquisitive, time-consuming modes of knowledge. Time is unreal, hence of no importance. No reason for hurry.

Why idealize being present-oriented? The present time is good. Whatever is natural is good, and it is natural that the present should be good. Each present is as good as it can be. It cannot be other than it is. So one should enjoy the present. Happiness is always in the present. Even those who believe that happiness lies in the future will have to enjoy it as present when it arrives if they are to enjoy it at all. There is no way to enjoy anything except in a present. Since the present time is enjoyable, there is no need to hurry.

4) Europeans tend to want to change things. Indians tend

to regard change as illusory. Chinese experience change as natural.

Why should anyone want to change things? If we expect the future to be better than the present, then some change will have to occur between the present and the future. Since we want things to be better, we will have to try to make them better (otherwise we will be frustrated). There can be no progress without change. So we ought to try to make changes. How should we do this? Ideally in all ways. First we should seek to improve our own selves. Become educated, more educated, better educated. Then we seek to improve others: our children. Educate them. Christians send missionaries. Why? To improve the religion of others. Europeans fight wars? Why? To make things better. For example, many World War I soldiers were inspired by the wartime slogan: "Fight to make the world safe for democracy." Today Americans still feel obligated to help the underdeveloped, and developing, nations of the world. Billions of dollars are expended for scientific research. Why? We expect that the result will help to change things and, optimistically, to make them better.

Why believe that change is illusory? If ultimate reality is eternal, it does not and cannot change. Therefore change is not ultimate. If ultimate reality is good, its goodness cannot be changed or improved. Thus to believe that things can be made better really is to mistake what is illusory for what is real. The only change which can bring genuine improvement is that in which one escapes completely from the illusion of change into intuition of *nirvana*, eternal intrinsic value, by an act called *mukti* (liberation). The "Days and Nights of Brahman" are merely the appearance and disappearance of illusion. The "Law of Karma," which operates only in the illusory realm, determines one's experience of suffering in accordance with his willfulness to change things. *Hinsa*, violence, is willfulness, or will to change. *Ahinsa*, nonviolence, is willingness to refrain from trying to change things

Why accept change as natural? Because that is the way it appears. The sun rises, and the sun sets. Day is followed by night; then night is followed by day. There is a time to sow and a time to reap; then again there is a time to sow and a time to reap. One becomes hungry, and eats; and then again one becomes hungry, and eats. Nature (*Tao*) consists of changes; initiation (*yang*) is always followed by completion (*yin*), which is followed again by initiation and completion. What is natural is good, and natural changes are good. Hence it is good to be born, good to be young, good to be old, and good to die. Evil consists in meddling with nature's way. When the young act as if they were older, and the old act as if they were younger, then trouble occurs. "Those too eager for activity soon become fatigued...What is against Nature dies young."[11]

5) Europeans idealize production of goods. Hindus idealize non-attachment. Chinese idealize enjoyment of life.

Why idealize production of goods? If desires are to be satisfied in the future, then we should attend to the means needed to bring about such satisfaction. Future orientation implies a need for present attention to means to future ends or goals. Which values are most important? Means or ends? If ends lie in the future and means are needed to achieve them, then present efforts should be devoted to such means. When people are observed to be preoccupied with means, they appear to regard means as more important than ends. The "work ethic" of farmers, manufacturers, businessmen and industrialists urges even greater efforts to produce more and better means.

John Dewey, American philosopher, called his philosophy "Instrumentalism," asserting that all values are instrumental and arguing against the "ends-in-themselves" theory.[12] Orthodox (Roman Catholic) religion places heaven after death and so obligates adherents to use Christ, the Church, the Sacraments and priests as aids, that is, means to achieve a future end. When Asian critics of American "materialism" express amazement at such preoccupation with means, I provide a reply: "Now that we have a generalized means, namely money, we believe that if you have enough money, then you can choose your ends. Therefore, get money." Even Asians understand this kind of reasoning. Somerset Maugham states the view in this way: "Money is a sixth sense; without it you cannot enjoy the other five." "Not having money is a way of being dead."[13]

Why idealize non-attachment? Every particular thing or value is temporary or illusory. To become attached to it as if it were real and a genuine value is to be misled. Granted that, if we cannot remove the veils of ignorance enshrouding our apprehension of the ultimate, we naturally become mistakenly attached to such things. If we cannot attain the ultimate end now, then we can at least try to live with some detachment to those things to which we are attached. Yogic practice aims at successive withdrawal of attention from objects, senses, thoughts, and even self-awareness; each such withdrawal involves withdrawing attachment. *Nirguna Brahman,* pure indistinctness as well as pure will-lessness, involves neither any distinct thing to be attached to nor any will to attachment. One can achieve such a goal only by removing attention from all distinctions and becoming completely disinterested, even disinterested in whether or not he reaches the goal. Attachment to means, even means to the end, distracts and prevents attention to the end. Therefore non-attachment is better than attachment.[14]

Why idealize enjoyment of life? Enjoyment of life should be a self-evident value. Those misled into preferring means to ends, that is, devoting the present to producing means useful in bringing about future ends, thereby postponing enjoyment of life, and those misled into preferring the end to means, that is, detaching interest in means so as to embody the end completely purified of means, are equally mistaken. Means and ends naturally involve each other, and both are necessary to the enjoyment of life. It is equally natural to work to produce food and then to enjoy eating it. Means and ends are not alien to each other. Both are present all of the time. *Yang* (initiation) as means to *yin* (completion) not only enables *yin* to be enjoyed when *yin* predominates, but *yin* (enjoyment of food) is a means to *yang* (desire to produce, and the production of, more food) which can also be enjoyed while it predominates. The Chinese spirit of willingness to enjoy life has been captured in English by Lin Yutang, *The Importance of Living*.[15] He writes convincingly that not to enjoy the present is to waste it.

6) Europeans project their ideal of willfulness as God. God created the world by an act of will, "Let there be light. And there was light." He was pleased with his handiwork and "saw that it was good." Later he destroyed much of his creation by an act of will, saving only Noah and his wife and pairs of animals from a devastating flood. For Jesus, God is love, willful love, concerned love, caring love, initiating love (love first without waiting to be loved). Orthodox theologians conceive God as omnibenevolent, that is, as wanting what is good, or best, for everyone. Hence he created a heaven and wills to get everyone there.

Hindus envision their ideal of will-lessness as *Nirguna Brahman*. The illusory world became manifest, not by an act of willful creation, but by eventual disequilibrium of the three *gunas, rajas, sattwa* and *tamas*. When *rajas guna*, the tendency to arouse attention, interest and action begins to dominate, evolutionary processes follow. But inevitably that which is aroused will finally become quieted, and quiescence will remain undisturbed because and so long as *sattwa guna* prevails. During a "Night of Brahman," nothing, and nobody, is anywhere.

Chinese depict their ideal of willingness as Tao. Tao acts naturally, and without exerting will. Yet will occasionally arises and causes action. Tao does not will to suppress such will or such action. Tao acts spontaneously, and willingly accepts its action as its own. "Whatever is produced, Nature accepts it for what it is. However it behaves, Nature lets it follow its own way."[16] Tao does not will to deviate from its own way. That is, it does not will to be more than it is nor less than it is with regard to any way that it is. Hence, it does not will to have more will than it has nor less will than it has.

Such ideals about ultimate reality (God, *Brahman* and *Tao*) are reflected also in human heroes, or ideal persons.

The European ideal man is a producer. He may be a farmer, a carpenter, a toolmaker, a builder, a scientist, an educator or a soldier. But he is at his best when he is producing his best results. Hence skill, intelligence and efficiency are among his highest virtues; yet he excels most when he becomes an inventor or (like God) a creator.

The Hindu ideal is a yogin. If one lacks capacity to practice *raja yoga* (withdrawing from life and progressing through the stages toward *samadhi*), then he may practice *karma yoga* (do good deeds or work for results without desiring rewards), *bhakti yoga* (devote self unselfishly to a cause or a deity), or *jnana yoga* (study scriptures, philosophy and Vedantic wisdom). Successful yogins do not normally remain in their bodies. But when one does, and becomes a *jivanmukti* (one who is aware of *nirvanic* quiescence while still alive), he is honored above all others.

The Chinese ideal man is harder to locate. In a sense, he is a person who lacks ideals, or at least idealizes lack of ideals. For when one is fully occupied enjoying the present, he has no need for attention to future enjoyments. For Lao-tzu, the ideal man has *teh*, the ability to follow his own nature without deviation, or without wanting to deviate (that is, without having ideals about deviating), from it. In another sense, he has ideals, but again these are ideals about living naturally. For Confucius, the ideal man tries to embody within himself *yi, jen, li* and *chih. Yi*, the best way of doing things, is for each thing and person to follow his own nature without deviating. Since each person is by nature social, his social nature should be followed in the best way also. *Jen,* good will, is the willingness that *yi,* the best way of doing things, should prevail socially also. *Li,* appropriate behavior, is the most efficient way to express one's *jen* in action. *Chih,* wisdom, is achievement of complete willingness to embody *yi, jen* and *li* in one's habits and attitudes. Since such perfect achievement cannot be expected, *chih,* etc., remain ideals. But, in either sense, the ideal man willingly accepts his own nature and has no desire to deviate from nature's way.

REASON

Again, differences in emphases can be summarized succinctly: Europeans idealize distinctness. Indians idealize indistinctness. Chinese accept both.

Exploration of these differences will be pursued relative to two kinds of illustrations:

A) Europeans idealize reason. Indians idealize intuition. Chinese accept apprehension.

B) Europeans idealize being realistic. Indians idealize being subjectivistic. Chinese accept being participatory.

Interrelations of these views with theory of the nature of existence and then with methodology will be developed for each of the two illustrations.

A) Europeans tend to idealize reason. Indians tend to idealize intuition. Chinese tend to accept apprehension.

1) Why idealize reason? Reason involves both a process and a capacity. As a capacity, reason is our ability to understand. As a process, reasoning is a method for achieving understanding. If we understand the nature of something, then we can predict how it will behave and so avoid evils which might result, or possibly use it for our benefit. Faith in our capacity to understand presupposes that the nature of things is understandable, and that what is understood is

rational also. To be rational is to involve ratios or relationships between things. So a mind can reason about things provided both mind and things are rational and involve similar relations.

How does reason understand? Or what do we do when we seek to understand the nature of anything? If it has a complex structure, we try to distinguish its different parts. Our method is analytic. If we cannot differentiate clearly between the parts without taking the thing apart, then we try to do so. For example, in elementary biology classes, we seek to understand the nature of life, and select as an example a worm or mouse or cat. First we kill the animal. Then we pickle it. Then we cut it up, and try to discover its digestive system, its circulatory system, its nervous system, its skeletal system, its muscular system, its reproductive system, etc. If we can draw all of these in full structural detail, then we feel that we have accomplished understanding. The more parts we have distinguished, and the more clearly we have distinguished them, the greater, we believe, is our understanding. Yet, the life has disappeared, and it cannot be reassembled from the parts drawn.

Why idealize intuition? Intuition grasps the unity of a whole. It does so directly. That is, there is nothing between an intuiting awareness and what is intuited. Reason, on the other hand, when it infers, proceeds from data or premises to conclusions, often passing through intermediate steps or stages. Whereas inferences may be mistaken, in intuition, or direct apprehension, nothing intervenes to make mistake possible. Hence, intuition can provide certainty because what is intuited is grasped all at once as a whole. When we intuit something, we do not take it apart and then try to put it back together as a whole again. We grasp its wholeness immediately. Is not intuition the best, as well as quickest and surest, way of knowing? Why not idealize it?

Why accept apprehension? Experience comes both as a whole and its parts. A thing and its structure are not two different things. Each thing, each *tao*, is a natural whole with its own natural parts. To see the parts separated from the whole is to miss something fundamental to what appears. To grasp the whole while ignoring the equally apparent parts is to ignore something essential to what appears. So, by accepting both the whole and the parts of whatever appears in experience, we are misled neither through seeking to understand a whole by analyzing and separating the parts from the whole nor through grasping the whole all at once as if it had no parts which are different from each other and from the whole. Such apprehension seems to be a less distorted, or undistorted, way of knowing.

2) What are some metaphysical accompaniments of idealizing reason? Seeking to understand the structure of anything by distinguishing its parts is often accompanied by the following presuppositions. What is definite and distinct is more real than what is indefinite and indistinct. The parts of a thing are more real than its whole, and differences between the parts are more real than their sameness as parts of a whole. Thinkers are not always clear about such presuppositions. But sometimes the tendencies involved are carried to extremes. For example, Plato's eternal Forms of things alone have perfectly real Being, since created beings embodying such Forms are deficient in reality, ranging downward in a scale from Being to Non-Being. Gerard Smith and Lottie H. Kendsierski assert that "No thing in existence can be indefinite...." "An existing being is a definite being; an indefinite being is another name for 'nothing'."[17] Greek atomism exemplifies the view that parts, or particles, that is, the smallest, hence uncuttable, particles alone are real.

What are some metaphysical accompaniments of idealizing intuition? Direct grasping of a thing as a whole presupposes reality of that whole. Such a presupposition is sometimes accompanied by the view that the whole is more real than its parts, and that sameness throughout the whole is more real than any apparent dieffrences, and that any indefiniteness and indistinctness present in the whole is more real than seeming definiteness and distinctness of parts, that unity is more real than plurality, and that what is unstructured is more real than what is structured. Such presuppositions have been carried to extremes. For example, Advaita Vedanta claims that *Nirguna Brahman* is pure indistinctness, pure indefiniteness, pure indifference, and so much so that even the distinctions between distinctness and indistinctness, etc., are not parts of it. Madhyamika Buddhism interprets *sunya*, the void, as completely void of distinctions, etc., including the distinction between *sunya* and suchness, that is, that which is void of distinctions and that which includes all distinctions. Theravada Buddhism refers to *bhavanga*, a perfectly undisturbed flux of being underlying mistaken beliefs in permanent things, which is utterly free from all distinctions, etc., whether temporary or permanent, between such beings. Even dualistic Samkhya pictures each liberated *purusha* (soul in *kaivalya*) as awareness purified of distinctions, and *prakriti* (nature) as somehow more perfect when its evolved manifestations have returned to their quiescent, more potential, unmanifest state. Although particular intuitions normally involve both distinctness and indistinctness, the ideal intuition is that of ultimate reality, experienced as *nirvana*, which is without (*nir*) distinctions, disturbances, or tendencies (*vana*, literally "wind").

What are some metaphysical accompaniments of accepting apprehension? When things, a person, a flower or a vista, for example, appear in experience, the willingness to believe that they are as they appear leads to seeing them as both wholes and parts, as both distinct and indistinct, as both alike and different, and as both permanent and changing. Each thing has its own nature (*tao*). Each *tao* is a natural whole with its own natural parts and its own natural way of proceeding. Things grow. Whether a person, a flower, a day or a year (four seasons), each thing has its beginning, grows to its fullness, declines, and finally dies or ceases to be. Each stage is different from and distinguishable from its predecessor and successor; yet it is still the same thing (*tao*) which proceeds through the stages. Each *yang* (initiation) is distinct from its *yin* (completion) both in general and in particular (see hexigrams of the *I Ching*). Acceptance of the reality of both sameness and difference apparent in our apprehensions is manifest even in the Confucian "golden rule": It does not imply that people are all the same ("Treat others as you are treated" or "Treat others as you would like to be treated") but that they are both the same and different: "Treat others as you would like to be treated if you were that person (who is also different from you)."

3) What are some methodological accompaniments of idealizing reason? If existing things have structures with real parts which are genuinely different from each other, our aim, in seeking to understand, is to discover such structure, such real parts, such genuine differences, and this aim entails seeking clear definitions of our terms, clear demarcation of boundaries and limits, and perfect truth as correspondence of clear and distinct ideas with definite structures and boundaries. Faith in reason leads to idealizing, not just forms of things, but also forms of processes. Recurrent forms, especially when regularly recurrent, are regarded as uniformities. This faith is epitomized in idealizing the "principle of the uniformity of nature": When given antecedents cause a consequence, then, when exactly the same antecedents recur again, they will cause exactly the same consequence. Thus universals, principles, laws are sought, both inductively and, when possible, deductively. Although controversy over the nature of universals has continued, and will continue, for a long time, European thinkers (Platonists excepted) have tended to regard the plurality of particulars in which universals are embodied as either more real than or equally real with such universals. And each universal (and here Platonists are included) is different from, and distinct from, every other universal. Even when looking for samenesses, idealizers

of reason tend to be looking for different samenesses. Classification of kinds is a natural accompaniment of distinguishing a plurality of parts and rigorous defining of boundaries.

What are some methodological accompaniments of idealizing intuition? If ultimate reality is pure indistinctness, the way to grasp it is directly and not through its opposite, namely, distinctions. So the method of yogins is a dual one: not merely to eliminate all desire (will) as previously indicated but also to eliminate all awareness of distinctions. Although distinctions do appear in consciousness, all are illusions mistaken for realities in ordinary experience. So the yogin must eliminate from awareness not merely the distinctions between things as objects, but also between different kinds of sensation, between different ideas, and between self or subject and all objects. The seeker must seek to annihilate even himself as seeker from awareness, for the goal he seeks, *nirvana*, pure indistinctness, contains no distinction between self and object. If the yogin cannot eliminate such distinctions from his awareness without having the capacity to eliminate them, he must achieve mastery over them so that he can eliminate them at will. Varieties of methods, or *yogas*, or *margas*, are recognized. But all require that the yogin achieve the goal only by eliminating both—any distinction between himself and the goal and any will to achieve it. The goal, *nirvana*, is *chit*, awareness or intuition purified of distinctions, *sat*, being purified of differences, and *ananda*, bliss purified of desire.

What are some methodological accompaniments of accepting apprehension of whatever appears? The nature (*tao*) of each thing has both wholeness and parts. By accepting the nature of things as they appear, one does not seek to abstract the parts from the whole, nor does he seek to abstract the whole from its parts. "If Nature is inexpressible, he who desires to know Nature as it is in itself will not try to express it in words. To try to express the inexpressible leads one to make distinctions which are unreal."[18] By accepting the nature of processes as they appear, one does not seek to abstract the permanent from the changing nor the changing from the permanent. The same *tao* begins, grows, declines, and ends, and yet such *tao* becomes different as it grows, declines and ends. Natural cycles appear as we observe the regular rounds of day and night, spring, summer, fall and winter, birth, growth, decline and death, and the rise and fall of dynasties. Yet days and nights differ in length and occurrences, years differ as seasons are hotter or colder, wetter or dryer, longer or shorter, and lives differ in vitality, maturation rates, and lengths, and dynasties in power and endurance. Hence, the regularities are themselves irregular, seeming uniformities are observed to recur with differences, and the distinctions between stages often are very indistinct as they flow into each other (day passes into night as the sun sets gradually, through evening and twilight). Instead of expecting rigid uniformities, the Chinese tend to look for analogies. The *I Ching* (*Book of Changes*), consisting of sixty-four analogies, is available for the ambitious. Like the water buffalo, the Taoist follows his own nature and permits every other thing to follow its own nature; he accepts his own nature as it appears to him and accepts the natures of other things as they appear in his apprehension. Hence, methodologically, he is not unduly concerned about seeking distinctions or about eliminating distinctions. "There is no distinction between rational and irrational thought in the history of Chinese philosophy."[19]

4) Implicit in the three differing emphases regarding ideals about reason, intuition and apprehension, and their accompaniments, metaphysical and methodological, are some logical differences.

European thought, structured in part by Euclidean geometry and Aristotelian logic and developed through Boolean algebra and symbolic logic, has sharpened its notion of negation in terms of an ideal called "an excluded middle." Between *a* and *not-a* there is nothing; or *a* and *not-a* have nothing in common. This ideal is often formulated in terms of "exclusive disjunction": "*X* is either *a* or *not-a*, but not both." The sharpness of this distinction between *a* and *not-a* has enabled thinkers to define and clarify ideas, inferences, and systems with perfect precision, and has made possible developments in science, technology, and engineering which astound all.

Indian thought, when regarding ultimate reality as without distinctions, has idealized *Nirguna Brahman* as the negation of all negation. Since any distinction involves two things which are distinct from, and hence not, each other, negation is involved in every distinction. To eliminate all distinction is to eliminate all negation. Ideally, no statements can be truly made about *Nirguna Brahman*, because all statements involve distinctions. But demands by inquirers have been met with a formula which can be used for comparative purposes. Of *Nirguna Brahman* (and the same holds for any thing taken as having ultimate reality) one may say: "It (X) is neither *a*, nor *not-a*, nor both *a* and *not-a*, nor neither *a* nor *not-a*." This "principle of four-cornered negation,"[20] which one can find repeated copiously in the Pali *Pitakas*, provides a clue to something fundamental about Indian mentality.

Chinese thought, accepting both parts and wholes, and their distinctness and indistinctness, as apprehended, have come to idealize a "both-and" logic. Not only does the nature of each thing have its wholeness (*tao*) but each *tao* consists of its opposing parts *yang* and *yin* which, though distinguishable, are inseparable from it and, though distinguishable within it, are not distinct from it. Since distinguishable stages in any cycle of changes shade into each other, such that the borderline between them is not distinct, we may say that Chinese tend to idealize distinctions which are not too distinct. Neither idealizing opposites (*yang* and *yin*) as having nothing in common, since they have both *tao* in common and their partial indistinctness from each other, nor idealizing that which opposites have in common (*tao*) as itself purified from distinctions, they find themselves accepting a "both-and" logic: Not only does each thing that exists, x , have both *yang* and *yin* (*a* and *non-a*), which is itself both distinguishable from and yet not completely distinguishable from them, but also each opposing part (whether *yang* or *yin*) has its own opposing parts which, as diagramed by trigrams or hexigrams, form series of tiers, each of which, when added to the first, exemplifies reapplication of the "both-and" logic.

These emphases, epitomized in three formuli, have been symbolized by diagraming variations on three circles. The rationalist ideal of an excluded middle may be represented by a circle divided exactly in half, with one half pure white and the other half pure black. The Indian ideal of distinctionless *Nirguna Brahman* has been captured in the seventh of the "Ten Cow-Herding Pictures," a series of Zen paintings designed to illustrate how one needs to achieve *nirvana* before returning to practice Zen in everyday life. The Chinese ideal of *Tao* consisting of *yang* and *yin* is depicted in the well-known *Tao* symbol; when drawn correctly, the light (*yang*) and dark (*yin*) portions of the symbol are so arranged that a string placed on any diameter will include some of both, so that swinging such a string around over all diameters will never fail to include some of both. In case any doubt remains about the intent, some designers add a spot of light in the middle of the dark portion and a spot of dark in the light portion. "Both-and" prevails over the entire symbol.

Either *a* or *not-a* but
not both
Excluded middle
Clear distinctions

Neither *a*, nor *not-a*, nor both
a and *not-a*, nor neither *a* nor
not-a. Fourcornered negation
purified of all distinctions

Both-and
Distinctions which
are not too distinct

The differences in emphasis regarding reason, intuition and apprehension idealized in European, Indian and Chinese cultures are very aptly symbolized by the foregoing three circles. Part of the thesis of this essay is that whoever fails to detect these differences in emphases fails to comprehend something fundamental about the differences between the philosophies of the three civilizations. Awareness of these differing emphases provides a significant clue to the varying ways in which typical mentalities develop. The symbols may be taken as clues not merely to differences in ideals regarding logics, but also regarding theory of reality, theory of knowledge, theory of value, aesthetics, ethics and religion, and even social and political theory. For example, the Korean flag, which consists of the *Tao* symbol encircled by three trigrams, is at once a living and forceful political symbol and an ancient and revered religious symbol. And, whether or not Koreans are greatly exercised about them, logical, metaphysical, epistemological, axiological and aesthetic issues and tendencies toward their solution are also symbolized in their flag.

B) Our second kind of illustration of difference in emphases pertains to issues involved in making subject-object distinctions or, better, subjective-real distinctions. Europeans tend to idealize being realistic. Indians tend to idealize being subjectivistic. Chinese tend to accept being participatory.

1) How do Europeans idealize being realistic? Reason not only distinguishes between one thing and another, between parts and whole, and between a thing and its structure, but also between a knower and what is known. Not only do trees, rocks, animals, sun, moon, stars and other persons appear to exist really, that is, in the sense that they exist whether or not they appear to anyone, but also in thes ense that there is more to each thing than appears. Analytic methods, as they have progressed, not only have revealed finer distinctions, more intricate structures and smaller parts, but have confirmed a faith that reality lies behind the appearances of

objects. What once appeared to be a hard rock, when taken apart, appeared to be composed of numerous compounds. These were successively analyzed into numerous molecules, then atoms, and then subatomic particles, which continue to multiply as research proceeds. No one has ever seen an atom, much less a subatomic particle. Yet belief in them is required if our analyses, which have yielded sufficient understanding to enable us to put men on the moon, are correct. Ultimate reality lies behind the appearances, and remains, and will continue to remain, invisible.

This ideal of the invisibility of ultimate reality did not await the development of modern physics. God, creator and sustainer of the world, is also invisible. No one, supposedly, has seen God. Even Moses, who obtained a Convenant from God, did not see God. God as a perfect being is inaccessible to imperfect vision. God is knowable through his manifestations, his creations, and perhaps revelations. But God is a reality which is behind the appearances of objects.

How do Indians idealize being subjectivistic? Reality (*Brahman* as *Atman*) underlies the appearance of self. The real self, thought of as soul (*jiva, purusha, atma*), is invisible, inaudible, intangible, etc., and thus cannot be apprehended by any of the senses; and yet it is the source of self-awareness (*ahamkara*), ideas (*manas*), the senses (*indriyas*), and objects (*vishaya*). Without a self, which has the capacity to be aware of objects, there could be no awareness of objects, and thus no objects of awareness. Objects of awareness depend upon awareness, and awareness depends upon a self which is aware. A self both intuits itself and intuits the objects of which it is aware. No objects of knowledge, no matter how diverse, multifarious or complex, can be without being objects for some self or subject. Hence, the subjective is the foundation of all knowledge of all objects. Ultimate reality is to be found not in appearances but in disappearances. Only when waking consciousness gives way to dream consciousness and then to dreamless consciousness does the subject-object duality disappear. But *Atman* itself is as different from dreamless consciousness as dreamless consciousness is from dream consciousness; it is unconscious awareness, awareness in which there is not even awareness of self.

How do Chinese accept being participatory? A person finds himself in company with other persons in a house on land which extends toward the horizon and in air which extends to the sky. Why should he not accept himself as he appears? Why should he look behind the objects (house, land, sky) for some hidden reality (atoms or God)? Why should he look behind himself as looking to find some hidden invisible soul? Why not accept what is directly apprehendable in appearances as real? If one does, then the distinction between appearance and reality is not an important one. Hence, there is no need to look for such reality in either direction, that is, behind objects or behind self. Naive realism, the philosophy of the common man, or ordinary people, in all cultures, may be subject to criticisms; but even the critics adopt it in their everyday behavior. Each particular *tao* participates in *Tao*; why should one expect to have it any other way?

2) What are some metaphysical accompaniments of idealizing being realistic? The outer is regarded as more real than the inner. What lies behind the appearances of objects (atoms, or God, etc.) is more real than the objects as they appear. Although the implication is not a necessary one, the search for reality behind the appearances of objects tends to signify that what is being searched for is more real than the searcher, or the self doing the searching. Truth, as conformity of ideas with real things, is subjective; it depends for its existence upon conformity of ideas with real things; reality does not depend for its existence upon conformity with subjective ideas. Ideas can be mistaken; but not external reality. But, to the extent that we can know the truth about things, we must attain it by investigating reality which is outside ourselves and which lies behind appearances.

What are some metaphysical accompaniments of idealizing being subjectivistic? The inner is regarded as more real than the outer. Objects which depend upon subjects are less real than the subjects upon which they depend. Subjects (*ahamkara*) are less real than the real self (*atman*) underlying self-awareness. The yogin does not seek truth as correspondence of ideas with real things; he seeks to realize the identity of his individual self with the universal self (*atman*). When awareness of such identity is attained, the result is not truth, in the foregoing sense, but an intuition of reality itself. Reality itself (*sat*) is sought, not truth about, and thus different from, reality; the "truth" which the yogin seeks is *satya*, a going toward (*ya*) reality (*sat*). But it is going in an inward direction to an inner reality.

What are some metaphysical accompaniments of being participatory? When one is naively realistic and accepts *apparent* realities as apparent *realities*, he does not look elsewhere for reality. Reality is not something which one has to "look for" or "go in search of." One accepts himself as a reality (a *tao*) participating with other realities (*taos*) in a larger reality (*Tao*). One does not need to bother himself with metaphysical quests. One's own inner nature (one's own *tao*), with its hunger and feelings of satisfaction, is real. Other persons who are outside oneself (other *taos*) are real. And both participate in *Tao*, or are within *Tao* which is also within each *tao*. Thus *Tao* is both inside and outside each *tao*. There is no need to regard the outer as more real than the inner nor the inner as more real than the outer. Acceptance of both inner and outer as real follows from accepting apparent participation of *taos* in *Tao*.

3) What are some methodological accompaniments of being realistic? One will look for reality outside self and behind appearances of objects. He will seek to be "scientific." The "scientific method" requires that one attempt to "be objective." That is, one will not permit subjective factors, such as wishes, preferences or prejudices, to influence his investiga-

tion, for to do so is likely to produce conclusions which are biased or even false. Since invisible atoms do not lend themselves to direct observation, some method of indirect contact must be devised. So search for knowledge of reality requires tools, instruments, machines designed for this purpose. Rulers, scales, watches, meters, guages, calipers, thermometers, speedometers, electroencephalograms, microscopes, telescopes, electron microscopes, etc., are needed. Now that we have betatrons, and meson facilities, we are looking for still more intricate and powerful mechanisms for detecting and measuring the dynamic entities, or events, which constitute invisible reality. The more complex, intricate and quantitative, the greater the need for relying on measurement and thus upon mathematics. Now we depend upon computers, "second, third and fourth generation" computers, and computer complexes.

Such methods presuppose that measurement of reality is possible. The best way to understand it is by measuring it: its length, weight, size, speed, growth rate, etc. Scientific research often depends upon measuring techniques so much that whatever cannot be captured by such techniques cannot be taken into account. This problem has begotten the slogan: "If it can't be measured, it doesn't exist." Now, when computers are employed increasingly for such measurements, do we find ourselves saying: "If it can't be computerized, it doesn't exist"? Or, further, if there are a limited number of programming systems, logics or languages, such as Fortran, will we be operating scientifically as if: "If it can't be Fortraned, it doesn't exist"?

What are some methodological accompaniments of being subjectivistic? If the inner is more real than the outer, one who seeks ultimate reality will direct his attention inwardly. In order to do this, he will have to reverse his normal habits of naive realism and scientific realism, if such have developed, and this will involve attempts to shut out stimuli from the external world and whatever attracts his attention to such external world. Yogins have discovered several standardized subjective lay ers to be explored, controlled and overcome in practice. Patanjali's "The Eight Limbs of Yoga" serves many as an ideal outline for such practice. These are: (i) Abstention (not injuring, not lying, not stealing, not being sensual and not being possessive). (ii) Devotion (to cleanliness, serenity, self-discipline, self-study and dedication to the ideal of supreme selfhood). (iii) Posture (undisturbed by tensions). (iv) Relaxation of breathing (steady and undisturbed). (v) Retraction of the senses. (vi) Fixation of attention (so that it will not wander). (vii) Fusive apprehension (distinctions between contents of consciousness disappear). (viii) Fully integrated consciousness (mind also becomes unconscious of itself as distinct from objects).[21]

The more unified awareness becomes, the more distinctness disappears. The self, ultimately, is pure unity, or at least is purified of all distinction. Hence, the self is immeasurable. It can neither be counted nor subdivided into countable parts. All supposed measurements of self are illusory. Measuring techniques not only are not necessary; they result in necessarily false views of ultimate reality.

What are some methodological accompaniments of being participatory? If each *tao* participates in *Tao* and both are genuine realities, one observes both similarities and differences between one *tao* and another and between each *tao* and *Tao*. That is, he can observe analogies. All years are alike in having four seasons; but in some years the summers are longer and in other years the winters are longer. All days are alike in having both day and night; but sometimes the days are longer and sometimes the nights are longer. So with lives, dynasties, flowers, and journeys. The *Book of Changes* (*I Ching*) is not a system of measurement; yet it can be used for purposes of predicting by means of observing analogies. When one accepts his own nature and follows its own ways, he does not need to look for reality behind objects and invent intricate techniques of measuring for doing so; and he does not need to look for reality behind his apparent self and to exert great effort in eliminating awareness of objects and of self.

Further methodological accompaniments of these three ways of idealizing are:

The realist seeks to understand what is behind the appearance of objects first and his self later, if at all. A European who wishes to understand himself may begin by studying physics, chemistry, biology and physiological psychology. These are ways of studying the foundational constituents of a self. The nervous system is explained sometimes in terms of mechanical models, such as a telephone system or, now, computers. Many college psychology laboratories have cages full of white rats. Why? Students study the behavior of rats. Why? Because men are like rats. We study other animals first so we can then better understand ourselves. Even those theologically inclined do the same; that is, believing that man is created in the image of God, who is the invisible power behind the appearance of objects, they seek to study the nature of God. If men are God-like, then the way to learn about ourselves is to study the nature of God first.

The subjectivist seeks to understand self first and other things, if at all, later. For if other beings are like us, then if we understand our own selves first we can understand them more easily. If we have feelings, hopes, fears, hunger, etc., then we can infer that other beings, such as rats, monkeys, cows and elephants, have similar feelings, hopes, fears, etc.

The participant finds himself and others both alike and different. Observing self-in-the-world as obvious, he does not feel compelled either to understand the world first so he can understand himself or to understand self first so he can understand the world. Where analogies appear between himself and a cow, both eat, drink and excrete, he can observe other analogies flowing from such similarities with differences. Confucius studied analogies observable in different families and kingdoms and concluded that the principle of reciprocity (*yang-yin*) operating naturally among men functions best when we also discriminate differences which occur in social situations: "Treat others (in the same way) as you would be treated if you were in their (different, or partly the same and partly different) shoes."

(4) Europeans project their ideal of reason as God. God, as omniscient, is perfectly rational. God, as omniscient, has all of the possibilities of existence as well as the details of all actual existences clearly in mind. Leibnitz expressed this idea by saying that God knows all of the possible universes which might be created and, being all-good, selected the best of all possible worlds when creating this one. God clearly knows all distinctions. God is never in error, either in perceiving or inferring. Though God is outside of both the world and of each person, God's knowledge of each worldly and personal event is complete.

Indians envision their ideal of intuition as *Nirguna Brahman*. *Nirguna* (distinctionless) *Brahman* (being) is *sat* (pure being), *chit* (pure awareness) and *ananda* (pure bliss). No distinction exists between *sat-chit-ananda (satchitananda)*. Hence *Nirguna Brahman* is the being of blissful intuition completely purified of all distinction. Though *Nirguna Brahman*, for Advaitins, is the only ultimate reality and is not different from *Atman* which is the being underlying all individual selves with their complex ideas experienced through countless reincarnations, these multitudinous distinctions do not inhere in it. "Omniscience" is intuition of ultimate reality, that is, of everything all at once without distinction.

Chinese depict their ideal of apprehending participation as *Tao*. *Tao* participates in all of its parts, that is, in all of the particular *taos*. Each particular *tao* participates in *Tao*. An unborn calf participates in its mother's body, and may have no awareness because there is no need for awareness of such participation. But when born, it soon opens its eyes, stands on its legs, and, being hungry, seeks milk from its mother. That it apprehends its mother and sucks milk is evident from its survival. The cow apprehends its calf as a somewhat independent offspring with its own nature. Such awareness which one thing has of itself and of others, and of similarities and differences from others, seems to be sufficient for natural growth. *Tao* neither reasons about perfect distinctions nor intuits purified being; *Tao* proceeds and such awareness as is needed by particular beings emerges in due course.

Such ideals about ultimate reality (God, *Brahman* and *Tao*) are reflected also in human heroes, or ideal persons.

The European ideal person is the specialist, one who knows both the general principles and the specific details about his field. He cannot, like God, know everything, but he tries to know everything about something. Whether with scientific understanding or practical know-how, the specialist aims to be an expert in dealing with real things and to be acquainted with alternative possibilities regarding the way things behave or develop.

The Indian ideal person is the yogin, one who seeks to eliminate distinctions between self and objects as well as between objects. Believing that all distinctions are illusory, he seeks to achieve that ultimate intuition of his identity with *Nirguna Brahman.* One who cannot practice yoga in ways which will bring him liberation immediately will pursue *gnana yoga* (study of scriptures or philosophy), *bhakti yoga* (selfless devotion to a deity), or *karma yoga* (constant doing of good deeds) as ways which will help him to achieve liberation later.

The Chinese ideal person is one who is enjoying life. He is enjoying life because he is accepting his nature and present circumstances as good without wanting them to be different than they are. Although I do not know whether cooks enjoy life more or less than other Chinese, the world-renowned excellence of Chinese cooking makes me wonder (perhaps this is wishful thinking) whether cooks are not first among the heroes of Chinese culture.

Concluding remarks are of two sorts. (i) While attending to details, the reader is likely to have forgotten that the foregoing hypothesis about differing emphases prevailing in each of the three civilizations has presupposed that more similarities than differences, biological and cultural, exist. (ii) Knowledge of these differing emphases may be useful to persons within each culture in better understanding his own culture by becoming aware of differing emphases elsewhere. Knowledge of these differing emphases may be helpful to those trying to understand persons from other cultures. Knowledge of these differing emphases may supply one with additional cultural riches from which to draw traits in shaping up his own unique personality. Knowledge of these differing emphases may provide insight into the problems to be faced, including cultural conflicts to be overcome, as people, living closer together on a shrinking globe, participate in the emergence of a more complicated world culture.

NOTES

[1]"Indian" includes. Buddhism as well as Hinduism. "Chinese" includes Korean and Japanese cultures. "European," which has Judaism, Christianity and Islam as typical religions, extends wherever these ideals have spread, obviously to North and South America. Hence, Islam in India and Marxism in China are still "European" and Buddhism in China is still "Indian."

[2]Unfortunately Rudyard's Kipling's long poem, which begins "East is East, West is West; And ne'er the twain shall meet," often has been quoted to "prove" differences, whereas the same poem ends by emphasizing sameness:

> *But there is neither East nor West,*
> *Border nor breed nor birth*
> *When two strong men stand face to face*
> *Though they come from the ends of the earth.*

[3]Further details of this hypothesis appear in my *The World's Living*

Religions, pp. 276-286, Dell Publishing Co., N.Y., 1964; Southern Illinois University Press, Carbondale, 1971.

[4]The foregoing sketch has been limited to examples drawn primarily from Christian-dominated traditions. Reason-versus-will debates occurred also among Jewish philosophers after being influenced by Greek philosophy and among Moslem philosophers whose influence upon Thomas Aquinas, for example, was partly responsible for the timing and intensity of the debate among Christian philosophers. Not only are the histories of the reason-will controversies among Jewish and Moslem philosophers rich and complicated in themselves, but they were further enriched by the mutual influences which Jewish, Moslem and Christian philosophers had on each other.

[5]Koran, Ch. 53, 1. 39.

[6]See my Philosophy of the Buddha, pp. 15ff, Harper and Brothers, N.Y., 1958; Collier Books, N.Y., 1962; Capricorn Books, N.Y., 1969.

[7]See my Tao Teh King by Lao Tzu, pp. 33, 45-48, Frederick Ungar Publishing Co., N.Y., 1958.

[8]Delacorte Press, N.Y., 1968.

[9]See my Bhagavad Gita: The Wisdom of Krishna, p. 46, footnote 29. Somaiya Publications, Ltd., Bombay, 1970.

[10]Advocates of each of the four ways to the goal, Karma Yoga, Bhakti Yoga, Jnana Yoga and Raja Yoga, in their mature forms involve Nishkama Yoga, acting to achieve results without regard for rewards. (See ibid., pp. 7-17.) Patanjali in Part III, Sutra 9, of his Yoga Sutras, says, "Desire of the mind to suppress disturbances is itself a disturbance of the mind which must also be suppressed before it can reach that state in which desire is completely suppressed." (Yoga: Union with the Ultimate, p. 126, Frederick Ungar Publishing Co., N.Y., 1961.)

[11]Tao Teh King by Lao-Tzu, p. 51.

[12]Theory of Valuation, p. 56, University of Chicago Press, Chicago, 1939.

[13]Quoted in Gerald Sparrow's How to Become a Millionaire, Anthony Blond, Ltd., London, 1960.

[14]Theravada Buddhists go even farther than Vedantists and depict the ultimate as complete impermanence, exemplified in their no-soul doctrine. They accuse Vedantins of retaining Nirguna Brahman as something to which we should retain attachment. They interpret attachment itself as evil, and believe that detachment can be achieved more fully if they do not seek attachment to (identification with) Brahman.

[15]John Day Co., N.Y., 1937.

[16]Tao Teh King by Lao-Tzu, p. 48.

[17]Philosophy of Being, p. 96. Macmillan Co., N.Y., 1961.

[18]Tao Teh King by Lao-Tzu, p. 11.

[19]Josephy S. Wu in a lecture at the University of New Mexico on 14 April 1972.

[20]P. T. Raju, "The Principle of Four-Cornered Negation in Indian Philosophy," *Review of Metaphysics*, Vol. 7, June 1954, pp. 698-713.

[21]Summarized from *Yoga: Union with the Ultimate*, pp. 94-125.

IV. TRUTH, SATYA, CHÉNG: A COMPARATIVE STUDY

"Truth" and "falsity" are peculiarly Western terms. We find no exactly equivalent terms developing in the early civilizations of India and China. But each civilization did develop its own ways of conceiving how persons know what is. These ways differ because each civilization developed its own conception of the nature of what is. I symbolize three major kinds of emphases regarding how persons know what is in three terms: Truth. Satya. Chéng.

A. TRUTH

Western civilization includes two major civilizations, one originating in the philosophies of ancient Greece and the other originating in the Hebraic tradition. Each civilization provided its own conceptions of truth and falsity.

Since Greek civilization stressed *logos* as a rational ordering principle in existence, its conceptions of truth and falsity emphasized order and regularity. Plato claimed that Ideas (*Ideos*), or eternal Forms, served as archetypes or models for all things. Three ideas, The Good, The True, and The Beautiful, the highest in an hierarchy of Ideas, permeate (are immanent in) all other ideas in the hierarchy. So The True is embedded in the Form (nature) of each kind of being. Beings created by a creator (*Demiurgos*) embody Forms imperfectly, thereby lacking something of their true being (nature). Thus truth is embedded in being. However, also the predicate of a true sentence states what is true of its subject (i.e., form).

Later, Logical Realists conceived truth as a property of a

proposition when the proposition corresponds with a fact. Both proposition and fact are regarded as timeless or eternal beings. How eternal beings participate in temporal sentences remains unexplained. But this does not bother mathematical realists who program high speed computers in ways believed to produce true results.

Aristotle, distinguishing between Form and Matter in existing beings, developed a formal subject-predicate logic based on a substance-attribute metaphysics. His theory of truth: "To say of what is that it is, and of what is not that it is not, is true."[1] My studies produced a somewhat similar view: "Truth is a property of a belief when what is believed to be is, and what is believed to be not is not."[2]

The Hebraic tradition originated a persisting theory of truth: "God is omniscient. Truth is what God knows." For humans, truth is what God (Jahweh, Allah) has revealed to humans in the Bible (Torah-Talmud, Koran).

B. SATYA

Many theories of truth have been proposed in India as well as in the West. I select the views developed in Advaita Vedanta as exemplifying something typical and pervasive in the thinking both of many philosophers and many other people.

Satya is intuiting identity with being. This intuiting may occur at two levels.

1. *With pure being.* For Advaita Vedanta, ultimate reality, *Nirguna Brahman*, is pure being. It has no parts, no beings. It has no forms, no natures. It has no movements, no time. It has no desire, no purpose. It has no ideas, no knowledge of objects. It just is (*sat*). But as *sat-chit-ananda* (being-awareness-bliss), it is also pure awareness, and pure bliss. Ultimate reality, *Nirguna Brahman*, is the being of blissful awareness.

Atman (an individual soul believing that it has its own being) is really *Brahman* suffering from an illusion (*avidya*) of being different from other beings and *Brahman*. Individuals have wants, experienced as lacks, or as desires not fulfilled. Any being aware of lacking awareness of pure bliss naturally desires to eliminate that lack. *Yoga* is intention and effort to eliminate awareness of difference from perfect bliss. *Yoga* (the ultimate purpose of all of various yogas) is effort to become united with, or identical with, or nondifferent from, *Nirguna Brahman*.

Belief that the nature of what is as pure being and that identity (non-difference) of self from such being, exemplifies what Westerners call "true belief." *Satya* is toward (*ya*) being (*sat*). As long as a self remains aware of its lack of identity with Brahman, it lacks something of its actual being. As long as it intends (and acts on its intentions) to remove any differences of itself (*maya*, "veils of ignorance") from *Brahman*, the yogin must be tending toward pure being. Since *Brahman* is desireless, the yogin must desire to become desireless, or freed from desire. *Atman* is *Brahman*. *Yoga* is *satya*.

2. *With the being of objects.* Persons have awareness (*prama*) of beings (*artha*) or things (*tattva*) as objects. Truth (*yathartha*) is intuiting identity of *prama* with *artha*. Knowledge (*jnana*) of objects is false (*avidya*) when an object, which is in awareness (*prama*), is regarded as independent of the knower. *Jnana-tattva* is intuiting a thing (*tattva*) as it is. *Jnana-tatva* is *yathartha*.

C. CHENG

Chéng (誠), absolute sincerity or absolute certainty, is an attitude of willingness to accept what is as it is. It is confidence that what appears is as it appears. It is awareness without doubt.

Chéng is intuitive trust that existence (*Tao*) is self-sufficient, enduring, and reliable. *Tao* includes custom and tradition. What appeared to ancient Sages remains revered as reliable knowledge. The *I Ching* continues to be trusted as revealing kinds of conditions and processes in Nature. Analogical inferences tend to be accepted as reliable until predicted results do not occur.

The problem error occurs as deviations from *teh* and *ho*, for example, when either *yang* and *yin*, initiation and completion, are excessive. Any deviation, such as trusting too much or doubting too much, disappears as the process proceeds. It can occur when wanting too much of anything and when being too satisfied when more is needed. But *Tao* proceeds as a Way that overcomes deviations in doubt and certainty by proceeding in ways of reversing itself ("Reversal is the way of *Tao*"), because opposing tendencies, *yang* and *yin*, are opposites involving mutual immanence.

Although discussions of the "rectification of names" as appropriate to actualities as they appear is accepted as necessary practically, confident acceptance of the reliability of nature is generally regarded as a precondition of knowing. "Whenever in observing things there is doubt and the mind is uncertain, then external objects are not apprehended clearly. When my thoughts are unclear, then I cannot decide whether a thing is so or not. ...If we are to have such true knowledge of things, we must first not allow our mind to be uncertain."[3] "He who possesses *Chéng* is he who, without effort, hits what is right, and apprehends without the exercise of thought."[4]

Chéng is not an eternal or timeless Platonic Form embodied in created things. It is not a property of a proposition corresponding to a fact. It is not a statement that what is is and that what is not is not. It is not a property of a belief that what is believed to be is and that what is believed to be not is not. It is not what God knows (although it is what the Sage knows). It is not identity with pure being, but it involves awareness of participation in the being and processes of Nature, in the being of

Tao, Nature's Way. It is not *maya*, illusion. It is not *satya*, a yearning for pure being, for it is already an awareness of the being of *Tao* which is the ultimate existence.

NOTES

[1]*The Works of Aristotle*, Vol. VIII, *Metaphysica*, tr. by W. D. Ross, Second Edition, p. 1011b. Oxford: The Clarendon Press, 1928.

[2]Archie J. Bahm, "The Organicist Theory of Truth," *The Southwestern Journal of Philosophy* (Fall, 1975): 197-201.

[3]*Hsun Tzu*, Ch. 21. Quoted in Fung Yu-lan, *A History of Chinese Philosophy*, Vol. I, p. 369. Princeton: Princeton University Press, 1952.

[4]*Chung Yung*, Ch. XX, 18. Quoted by M. Motegi in his *Meson and Chung Yung*, p. 17. Yokahama: Yokahama City University, 1963.

V. GOOD, ANANDA, CHUNG: A COMPARATIVE STUDY

The concepts "good" and "bad," conceived as contradictory opposites, are peculiarly Western in origin. All civilizations have conceptions of values, positive and negative. But the concepts "good" and "bad," conceived as contradictory opposites, have been emphasized most in Western civilization. India and China have developed emphases of their own. I symbolize three major kinds of value theories by three terms: Good. Ananda. Chung.

A. GOOD

Western civilization includes two major civilizations, one originating in the philosophies of ancient Greece and the other originating in the Hebraic tradition. Each civilization provided its own conceptions of good and bad.

The Hebraic culture originated a theistic tradition conceiving God (Jahweh, Allah) as an eternal person who created the world by an act of will in "seven days." "Let there be light, and there was light." He created mankind, first one man, Adam, then Eve his wife ("from Adam's rib") in a Garden of Eden. God saw his creation as good. But he gave Adam and Eve free will, that is, ability to do what each wanted to do, even if the acts were prohibited by God. Tempted by Satan (whose creation is unexplained), they "ate of the fruit of the tree of knowledge."

87

This action constituted sin, willing to go against the will of God. Sin is the primary kind of evil in the theistic tradition.

Will is the primary characteristic of God and free will is a primary characteristic of persons. God is assumed to be good and that God's will is good and that what God wills is good. Paradoxes inherent in the tradition include the presence of evil in what is created as good Implied is the assumption that free will, ability to choose between doing good and evil (between what God wills and what persons will when they will differently) is somehow better than a world in which persons are created in ways that they always will what is good.[1]

Life on earth involves enjoyments and suffering, but the best life for those doing God's will is reserved for Heaven, a place where God dwells, and where persons who get there are privileged to be with God and to enjoy being with loved ones. Persons sin, and some have their sins forgiven. Others who must suffer for their sins are assigned to Hell, a place of extreme anguish. Some theologians claim that such suffering implicitly involves the glory of God, when conceived as perfectly Just, because He justly punishes sin, caused by willfulness contrary to the will of God.

Good is God, is God's will, is God's will for humans.

Since Greek civilization stressed *logos* as a rational ordering principle in existence, its conceptions of good and bad emphasized order and regularity. Plato claimed that Ideas (*Ideos*), or eternal Forms, served as archetypes or models for all things. Three Ideas, The Good, The True, and The Beautiful, the highest in the hierarchy of Ideas, permeate (are immanent in) all other ideas in the hierarchy. So The Good, which Plato regarded as the highest of the three, is embodied in the Form (nature) of every being. Beings created by a creator (*Demiurgos*) embody Forms imperfectly. Hence, each thing, although essentially intrinsically good, may lack goodness in various ways and degrees.

Western civilization also developed theories opposing Platonic Formalism by claiming that intrinsic good consists in feelings of enjoyment and intrinsic evil consists in feelings of suffering.

(1) Hedonism: Some Greek philosophers claimed that humans naturally seek pleasure, and that pleasures are good and pains are bad. Hedonism asserts that the goal of life is happiness, or achieving the most pleasure with the least pain. Later Hedonists, Jeremy Bentham and John Stuart Mill, adopted Hedonism as a social philosophy.

(2) Voluntarism, the theory that good consists in the feeling of satisfaction of desire, and evil in the feeling of frustration, is a world-wide common sense view. It finds many advocates in Western civilization, and is exemplified in the philosophy of my teacher, DeWitt H. Parker: "Desire is the only basis of value: value itself does not exist until desire is being satisfied."[2] Evil consists in feeling frustrated.

(3) Romanticism, the view that intrinsic good exists in the feelings of desire, or desireousness, is exemplified in feelings of eagerness, enthusiasm, avidity, lust, hope, and even anger and rage. When satisfaction terminates desire, it destroys desire, and so functions as evil. Feeling diminishing desireousness is bad, and apathy, as absence of desire, is intrinsic evil.

Each of these theories distinguishes between good and bad as opposites, and between ends and means, ends-in-themselves and means to ends, or intrinsic values and instrumental values, as did the Formalist, Aristotle: "The essence [essential Form] contains par excellence what is best in anything, and it is better for a thing to be desirable in itself than to be desirable for something else."[3]

For Hedonists, intrinsic good consists in pleasant feeling. Anything causing pleasant feeling is an instrumental good. For Voluntarists, intrinsic good exists while a person enjoys feeling desire being satisfied, and whatever contributes to such feeling, including desires themselves and objects of desires, and whatever engenders desires and makes objects desirable, is instrumentally good. For Romanticists, intrinsic good consists in feeling desirous, and whatever contributes to such feeling is instrumentally good.[4]

B. ANANDA

Many theories of value have been proposed in India as well as in the West. I select the views developed in Advaita Vedanta as exemplifying something typical and pervasive in the thinking of many Indian philosophers and as persisting as an emphasis for centuries.

Nirguna Brahman, ultimate reality, is *sat-chit-ananda*, being-awareness-bliss. Pure being, pure awareness, and pure bliss are identical in their purity. All else is *maya*, illusion, because apparent incarnation of such pure being diminishes its purity, and thus the quality of its being, awareness, and goodness. Progressive incarnation degenerates such purity by stages (e.g., *Ishwara, Trimuti, Vishnu, Krishna*, etc., including humans, animals, plants, earth, etc.). No evil exists, but progressive diminution of the ultimate purity appears as progressive increase in evil.

Yoga, all efforts to unite the soul with Brahman, is really intention to remove "veils of ignorance" preventing a person from being aware of what a person (*atman*) really is, i.e., *Brahman*. *Atman* is *Brahman*. *Yoga* is intention and effort to achieve intuitive awareness of identity of one's being with being.

Indian culture often recognizes four major kinds of value: *kama* (love), *artha* (wealth), *dharma* (duty), and *moksha* (liberation from *maya*). Philosophers account for all human and other natural functions of existing in terms of these values. All are normal illusions that become eliminated when a person achieves *moksha*, usually only in death. Some precocious yogins may achieve *mukti*, a condition of pure being, while still alive. Theravada Buddhists claim that some *arahants* (monks practicing yoga) achieve *nibbana* (*nirvana*) while still embodied. *Nirvana* (no-wind) is awareness of being undisturbed by anything, i.e., is awareness of pure blissful being.

C. CHUNG

Chung (中), is a concept of comprehensive harmony of existing beings and tendencies actively enduring and embedded in the natures of the world (*Tao*) and of persons (*taos*). Its endurance is continuingly unchanged (*yung,* 庸) and thus constantly reliable.

Chung exists both as an undisturbed steady *equilibrium* in which disturbing and opposing tendencies are kept in balance and as a dynamic *harmony* in which opposing tendencies blend together in organized wholes. *Chung* is able to continue to exist as harmony because it exists also as stable equilibrium, the nature of each tendency being immanent in the nature of the other.

I object to interpreting *chung* as a mean between extremes when the extremes are conceived as pre-existing the mean. When *Tao* proceeds on its Way, it embodies *chung* as its ability both to permit deviations within its nature as a mean and to retard them from going to extremes.

Chung permeates existence and experience by embodying many distinguishable constituents within its comprehensive harmony. These include:

Teh (德) is intelligence, or the ability of *Tao*, and each *tao*, to maintain its nature, or to continue to act in a way that its self-activity maintains its nature without deviating. Two ways of deviating are those within its nature and those related to other natures. Within a nature, *teh* (德) is the ability to resist both temptations to advance (*yang,* 陽) too much and to rest (*yin,* 陰) too much in any natural self-activity. In relations to other natures, *teh* is the ability to resist both imposition of any deviating influences by others into one's own self-active nature and any intentional effort to impose one's influences upon others that will cause them to deviate from their own natural self-activities.

Ho (和) is social intelligence, or the ability of persons in groups to live together harmoniously. Each person having *teh*, or personal integrity, naturally intends to develop and express one's own personal nature and interests (*tao*). But each person exists also as a member of a family group, and so has an essentially social nature (*shu*, 恕).

When associating with others, one's interests in maintaining one's personal integrity are not, by themselves, concerns for the interests of others. But each person's existing as a family member involves having interests in the natures (*taos*) and welfare (*shu*) of one's family members as integral parts of one's own nature and personal integrity.

Chung (忠) is conscientiousness in pursuing the welfare of others. Awareness of the mutuality of interests of self and of others commits one naturally to loyal devotion to their interests also. Pursuit of mutual welfare is aided by the principle of reciprocity, that people tend to treat each other as they are treated by others. Since refraining from interfering with the welfare of others is necessary for harmony, what you do not want done to you, do not do to others. Since helping others in developing their welfare is mutually beneficial, help others in ways that you will want them to help you. Since persons are different as well as alike in many ways, *chung* as conscientiousness is sensitive to differences as well as samenesses. So one should treat each person as one would like to be treated if one were that person. *Chung* involves sympathetic insight, as well as sympathy.

Jen (仁) is sympathy for humankind. It extends the natural altruism in family living (*shu*) to other living beings as participants in Nature's wholesome equilibrium and harmony. Persons have an instinctive commiserative response to the sufferings of others.

Yi (乂) is the best way of doing things. What is best for each person is to act naturally (*teh*), that is, without deviating from what is inherent in one's own nature and without causing others to stray from the ways of their own inner natures. What is best for each person is to act socially (*shu*) in ways contributing to social harmony (*ho*), so that the welfare of one's family and of humankind will prosper. Since habits and customs of social behavior become established for assisting persons and groups in doing what is best, *yi* involves concern for *li*.

Li (礼) is propriety or proper social behavior. It is the appropriate manner of overt behavior needed to express one's inner thoughts or intentions. Formulations of desirable social behavior have been many, exemplified by the "Great Norm" (1121 B.C.) which includes "Nine Categories," the Second of which is Five Activities, summarized as "appearance (respectfulness), speech (reasonable), seeing (clearness), hearing (distinctness), and thinking (profundity)."

Li is also regarded as the formal or structural nature of *Tao* and everything that exists. So the moral order participates in the cosmic order, and the principles of social harmony and cosmic harmony are mutually immanent. Groups develop customs, including rituals and ceremonies, which become traditional and these are available to those intending to be socially appropriate. Tradition has established the *Yi Ching*, interpreting sixty-four hexigrams serving as typical models for analogical interpretations of things and events.

Chéng (诚) is freedom from doubt about the nature and reliability of cosmic processes, including personal and social *yi* and *li*. It not only involves a willingness to accept things as they are, but also a sincere commitment to such acceptance. It is intuitive trust of what appears as obvious. It is experienced as at-home-ness in the universe and as participating in the world's comprehensive harmony.

Chih (智) is wisdom. It is unreserved commitment to wanting and doing whatever Nature (*Tao* and *taos*) presents as what needs to be done. Embodying *chih*, a person confronts life's problems willingly and responds to needs for one's services unquestioningly. This does not mean that one raises no questions, but only that no questions are raised about willingness to do what the situation requires.

Chung (中, is comprehensive harmony of all of the foregoing constituents. It is comprehensive in comprehending all of them; and more, because, as fully comprehensive, it includes all that exists. It is harmonious because it not only harmonizes them, but it is immanent in them in ways that make them immanent in it, and thus in each other.

It is not a mere mean between the extremes of its numerous constituent tendencies. It permeates *chi* (*qi*, 氣), the vital energy of dynamic Nature, as each forward moving tendency (*yang*) naturally tends toward more than it can attain, and thus toward an extreme. The extremes are products of its tendencies. It is not a mean between preexisting extremes.

Chung is not merely omnipresent in existence. Its nature is such that it cannot stop being what it is. It endures because it is unrelenting in its ability to restrain, or reverse, tendencies to deviate. It is constant (*yung*, 庸), and is often referred to as *Chung Yung* (中 庸). *Chung* is "a metaphysical principle of axiological perfection."[5]

Chung (中) is not God, a personal God who wills. It is not the will of God as a creator external to the world as created. It is not the good in the world, either as willed by God through creation or as God's will immanent in a world created by God. It contains no hell, or place for punishing sinners who fail to do God's will. It is not heaven as a place where individual souls remain eternally, enjoying either the company of their saved loved ones or the beatific vision of God's perfection.

Chung is said to be endowed by heaven. I have avoided using the term "heaven" because Western minds automatically interpret it theistically. Western theists cannot be naturalized enough to understand *Tao*. *Tao* is Nature. Nature functions through dynamic processes involving complementary opposites, generalized as *yang* (阳 , initiation) and *yin* (阴 , completion). *Tao's yang* nature is called "heaven." When *Tao* activates its nature, "heaven provides." In this way, *Chung* is provided by heaven. *Chung* is provided not only as man's moral nature (including all of the constituents listed above) but as something pervading all created existing. *Tao* is a moral universe. It needs no external creator God.

Chung is not a Platonic Form. It is everlasting, but not timeless or eternal in nature. It permeates all existing beings, including the forms of beings. But all existing beings embody processes of complementary opposites, not static forms. Plato's Demiurge embodies Forms imperfectly. Such lack of perfection is interpreted, not as positive evil, but as deficiency of good. But when a *yin* incompletely terminates a *yang* immanent in it, it also perpetuates something of the genuine nature of a *tao* proceeding through its next *yang*. The presence of *chung* in all processes assures its perpetuation.

Chung does not consist of good and evil as enjoyment and suffering. It does not have its primary location as feeling of pleasure, enthusiasm, satisfaction, or contentment. It is present in all these, but as a universal sustainer of the processes that make them possible and actual. It is not understood as the end of any means or as the means to any end, for, in it, both means and end persist as mutually immanent opposites. Persons experiencing *teh* and *ho* surely embody some feelings of enjoyment, and also some feelings of suffering when deviating from them.

Chung is not *ananda*, pure bliss, or the being of blissful awareness. Its existing in the world is not illusory, *maya*. *Chung* exists genuinely. It is not pure as something completely different from existing processes, because it permeates them as part of their being and nature. It participates in their *teh* and *ho*, and *yi* and *li*, and every deviation. A person does not need to practice *yoga*, effort to remove veils of ignorance which becloud one's awareness of identity with Brahman, which can become complete, often after many incarnations, only in death, extinction of the being of its illusory awareness. *Chung* is always present. There is much more to it than awareness, but it is present in awareness whenever persons become aware.[6]

D. SUMMARY

What do the concepts good, *ananda*, and *chung*, have in common?

To regard them all as theories of good is to interpret them with a Western bias. Comparative philosophers, seeking to understand the philosophies of different cultures, should try to understand them in terms of their own primary presuppositions. This task is difficult because it is practically impossible for any person to rise above one's culture completely. But the attempt can be made, and can be partially successful. Such partial success surely is worthwhile.

Some common features: All arise from human nature, biological and social, as natural developments. Hence, all are essentially human and cultural. Each performs a kind of function that is central and essential for an adequate philosophy of life. Each can offer suggestions to persons in other cultures for enriching their cultures by adopting ideas found beneficial. If and when a World Philosophy receives serious consideration by responsible officials, each will have a role to play in shaping up any final philosophy.

Good, Ananda, Chung: A Comparative Study

Good, *ananda*, and *chung* warrant consideration primarily in terms of their own cultural traditions in any adequate comparative philosophy.

NOTES

[1] A contradiction appears when theologians accept the Hebraic idea of happy families restored in Heaven with God and then claim, with Thomas Acquinas, that, since God is perfect in goodness and beauty, those preferring to give their attention to loved ones who are by nature imperfect (being saved "by grace" of Jesus' sacrifice) instead of to God (in a Beatific Vision) do not belong there.

[2] DeWitt H. Parker, *Human Values* (New York: Harper and Brothers, 1931): 24.

[3] *The Works of Aristotle*, tr. by W.D. Ross, Volume I, *Topica*, Book VI, 149b 38-40 (Oxford: The Clarendon Press, 1928).

[4] I have dealt with ends and means extensively in my *Why Be Moral?* Second Edition (Albuquerque: World Books, 1992): 56-90, 116-135, 308, 409-422.

[5] Thome H. Fang, *The Chinese View of Life* (Hong Kong: Union Printing Co., 1957): 52.

[6] Chinese philosophy has influenced my Organicism which is used here in my interpreting Chinese philosophy.

VI. THREE ZEROS: A COMPARATIVE PHILOSOPHY OF VOIDS[1]

"Zero" here means, not a number, but "void" or "complete absence." "Three zeros" refers to three kinds of complete ontological negation typically emphasized in the three great civilizations, Western, Indian, and Chinese. The three: absence of being, absence of difference, and absence of exclusion.

In the West, "zero being" is nonentity. "Being is; non-being is not."[2]

In India, being is, and cannot not be. Nirguna Brahman is pure being. As pure, it is void of everything else. Thus it is void of distinctions or difference. Its "zero" is zero difference.

In China, being is, and cannot not be. But being (*tao*) is permeated with distinctions (*yang* and *yin*). But its distinctions are never completely distinct. *Yang* and *yin* are mutually immanent in such a way that each embodies the other at least somewhat. *Yang* and *yin* never completely exclude each other. Opposition that is completely exclusive does not exist. But also complete opposition of opposition cannot be.

These three conceptions of ultimate ontological negations involve three different conceptions of logical negation: exclusive negation, negation of all negation, and negation of exclusion.

Indian logicians have emphasized contradictory opposition: "X is either *a* or *not-a* but not both." *A* and *not-a* have nothing in common. They are divided by an "excluded middle." "Nothing is both *a* and *not-a*."[3]

Western logicians have emphasized negation of all negations.

Three Zeroes: A Comparative Philosophy of Voids

"X is neither *a*, nor *not-a*, nor both *a* and *not-a*, nor neither *a* nor *not-a*."[4] Not only is all negation absent from Nirguna Brahman, according to Advaita Vedanta, but Nirguna Brahman is also non-different (*a-dva-ita*) from *maya*, all emanated or incarnated existence. Furthermore, absence of difference is claimed by Sunyavada, where Sunya, Void, is non-different from Suchness, existence as ordinarily experienced.

Chinese logicians emphasize negation of exclusion: "X is both *a* and *not-a*," or both *yang* and *yin*. They do not exclude opposition. "In fact, all distinctions naturally appear as opposites; opposites get their meaning from each other and find their completion only through each other." "The tendency toward opposition is ever-present." "Every positive factor involves its opposite factor."[5,6]

Comparing the three conceptions of absence with each other, we can observe that:

The Western conception of absence is absence of being, not absence of distinction or absence of exclusion.

The Indian conception of absence is absence of difference, including absence of exclusion, not absence of being.

The Chinese conception of absence is absence of exclusion, not absence of being or absence of difference.

NOTES

[1]This article is reprinted with permission from the *International Philosophical Quarterly*, Vol. XXXII, No. 4 Issue No. 128 (December, 1992), pp. 499–500.

[2]Parmenides, *On Nature*, Fragment 6. See Scott Austin, *Parmenides: Being, Bounds and Logic*, New Haven: Yale University Press, 1986, p. 161.

[3]Alfred North Whitehead and Bertrand Russell, *Principia Mathematica. Vol. 1, Second Edition* (London: Cambridge University Press, 1925), p. 217.

[4]See P. T. Raju, "The Principle of Four-Cornered Negation in Indian Philosophy," *Review of Metaphysics* 7 (1954), 694-713. See also A.J. Bahm, "Does Seven-Fold Predication Equal Four-Cornered Negation Reversed?" *Philosophy East and West* 30 (Oct. 1957-Jan.1958), 127-130. For additional examples, see

Dhirendra Sharma, *The Negative Dialectics of India* (East Lansing, Michigan State Univ. Press, 1970).

[5]A. J. Bahm, *Tao Teh King by Lao Tzu* (New York: Frederick Ungar, 1938), pp. 12, 15, 18.

[6]The Chinese conception of negation as negation of exclusion may be illustrated by the concept of *wu wei*, often translated into English as "inaction" or "non-action." But it means both action and non-action, since it means "action without effort" (Fung Yu-lan, *A History of Chinese Philosophy* [Princeton: Princeton University Press, 1952], vol. 1, p. 375) as when a thing's nature is self-active, neither acting on or being acted upon by anything else.

APPENDIX

COMPARATIVE PHILOSPHY AND WORLD PHILOSOPHY

Comparative philosophy, as the study of the major foundational presuppositions of Western, Indian, Chinese and other civilizations, is an important and substantial area of human understanding. It can also provide rich resources for the study of World Philosophy.

World Philosophy, as all of the ideas about which all persons can agree, because based on uniformities inherent in human nature and in the world in which persons live, will include some ideas embedded in the cultures of each civilization but only some. Each civilization embodies some beliefs that are false, as evidenced by their rejecting some true ideas in other civilizations.

My studies in Comparative Philosophy have motivated me to propose a methodology for considering World Philosophy. I propose that the United Nations University establish a Research Institute that will seek to discover all ideas about which all persons do agree. Such an Institute will have functions at four levels, distinguishable as I. Universal Agreements. II. Cultural Claims. III. Museums. IV. Freedoms:

I. Seeking to discover Universal Agreements is the primary purpose of the Institute. It will aim to ascertain all ideas needed for understanding human nature, including ways of optimizing human happiness.

II. Claims of all philosophies (of religions, civilizations, cultural traditions, political institutions, and persons) which regard themselves as having principles needed for World Philosophy should receive responsible consideration as candidates for Universal Agreements. Methods for testing for Universal Agreement will be needed.

III. Cultural traditions constituting human history can be regarded as worthy of memory, even cherished memory, by humankind even when recognized as no longer acceptable practically. Museums devoted to remembering ideas, institutions, and customs constituting human history seem desirable. Which of these should be prevented from becoming "extinct cultural species"?

IV. The Institute should recognize the rights of particular cultures and persons to have their "individual cultural differences" respected appropriately unless harmfulness to human welfare can be demonstrated.

I am especially concerned about the qualifications of persons committed to judging tests regarding Universal Agreements. They should have considerable understanding of the basic presuppositions of all of the world's cultures, as well as commitment to complete fairness in evaluating evidences and to the possibility and desirability of World Philosophy.

Some claimants will question whether Universal Agreements are possible. But human nature is the same in all human beings and all must have some beliefs about such universal nature. The world in which all live is the same in many ways (as demonstrated in many sciences). Each person must eat, sleep, breathe, exercise, excrete, desire, have feelings, experience enjoyment and suffering, and associate with others. Universal agreement about such essentials of living should be easy to ascertain.

Conflicts arise over cultural claims, and agreements about these are debatable. As examples, I propose three candidates for Universal Agreements, from three different civilizations, Western (Christian), Chinese (Confucian), and Indian (Gotama, The Buddha):

Love casteth out fear. Any person who has feared something and has then learned to love it no longer fears it.[1]

Treat each other person as you would desire to be treated if you were that person. This method gets the best results in associating with other persons.[2]

When you want what you do not get, you will be frustrated. To avoid frustration, avoid wanting what you will not get.[3]

Each of these claims involves a psychological principle that anyone can test for oneself. The possibility of some Universal Agreements should be easy to demonstrate.

Other cultural claims about the nature of self, society, and the universe, which disagree, continue to cause conflict. These need attention, and consideration. Some conflicts occur regarding common claims about the existence and nature of God or gods, about the origins of existence and of life and of persons, about life after death, about whether some races embody more divinity or intelligence than others, about which ancient scriptures are to be trusted most. These are claims that need consideration in seeking Universal Agreements that constitute World Philosophy.

NOTES

[1]*The Bible*, I John 4, 18.

[2]I interpret Confucius' principle, "Whatever you do not want done to you, do not do to others" (*Chung Yung*, 7), when more fully explained, as also implying positive interest in, and effort to intend sympathetic insight into, the nature of each other person.

[3]See my *Philosophy of the Buddha*, Fremont, California: Asian Humanities Press, 1993, p. 15. For details, see Chapters 1 and 4. See also my *The World's Living Religions*, Fremont, California: Asian Humanities Press, 1992, p. 100.

To assist in establishing a United Nations Research Institute, I have incorporated the Institute for World Philosophy, 1915 Las Lomas Rd. N.E., Albuquerque, N.M., 87106-3805, U.S.A.